Literacy Coaching

Literacy Coaching
Learning to Collaborate

Barbara J. Walker
Oklahoma State University

Allyn & Bacon

Boston   New York   San Francisco
Mexico City   Montreal   Toronto   London   Madrid   Munich   Paris
Hong Kong   Singapore   Tokyo   Cape Town   Sydney

Executive Editor: Aurora Martínez Ramos
Editorial Assistant: Jacqueline Gillen
Marketing Manager: Danae April
Production Editor: Janet Domingo
Editorial Production Service: Kathy Smith
Composition Buyer: Linda Cox
Manufacturing Buyer: Megan Cochran
Electronic Composition: Schneck-DePippo Graphics
Cover Administrator: Linda Knowles

For Professional Development resources visit www.allynbaconmerrill.com.

Between the time website information is gathered and then published, it is not unusual for some sites to have closed. Also, the transcription of URLs can result in typographical errors. The publisher would appreciate notification where these errors occur so that they may be corrected in subsequent editions.

Cataloguing-in-Publication data unavailable at press time.

Printed in the United States of America

10 9 8 7 6 5 4 3 2 1   13 12 11 10 09

**Allyn & Bacon
is an imprint of**

ISBN-10:   0-132-30128-8

ISBN-13: 978-0-132-30128-2

Dedication

To the women in my family:

My mother, who coached me through school, keeping her expectations high.

My sister, a dance teacher, whom I coached as she moved from teaching dance to teaching high school literacy.

My daughter, who keeps me levelheaded, and, sometimes, coaches me.

About the Author

 Barbara J. Walker is president of the International Reading Association (2008–2009) and professor of reading at Oklahoma State University, where she teaches courses in reading difficulties and literacy coaching. Dr. Walker has taught and coached teachers at two university reading clinics and in public schools.

Dr. Walker received her Ed.D. from Oklahoma State University in Curriculum and Instruction, specializing in reading difficulty. Prior to returning to Oklahoma, Dr. Walker was professor in the Department of Special Education and Reading at Montana State University, Billings. She was a reading specialist in the elementary schools of Stillwater, Oklahoma; organized and taught the college reading program at Vernon Regional Junior College in Vernon, Texas; and coordinated the educational program at the Hogar Paul Harris in Cochabamba, Bolivia.

Dr. Walker's research interests focus on reading teacher development, literacy coaching, and reading difficulties. Her publications include *Diagnostic Teaching of Reading: Techniques for Instruction and Assessment* (6th ed., 2008); *Techniques for Reading Assessment and Instruction* (2005); and *Supporting Struggling Readers* (2nd ed., 2003). Some of the book chapters that Dr. Walker has authored or co-authored include the following: History of

Phonics Instruction; Integration of Reading Assessment and Technology; and Collaboration in the Schools: A Theoretical and Practical View. She has authored or co-authored articles in *The Reading Teacher, Elementary School Journal, Journal of Teacher Education, Reading and Writing Quarterly,* and others.

Dr. Walker is a state, national, and international leader, having served on the board of directors of the International Reading Association, the College Reading Association, the Montana State Reading Council, and the Oklahoma Reading Association. Most important to her, however, is preparing teachers to work with struggling readers. In this capacity, she has helped more than 3,000 struggling readers improve their literacy.

Contents

Chapter 4

Gradual Release Model of Classroom Coaching 59

Chapter 5

Observations, Analysis, and Interpretation 73

Preface

Professional development to improve literacy instruction encompasses many possibilities. One of those possibilities is literacy coaching during classroom interactions. Literacy coaching is a powerful way to provide professional development for teachers and improve student learning. This book is based on a constructivist view of learning and teaching. In other words, learning and teaching are viewed as active processes in which teachers and students formulate their understandings. Further, the focus of this book is what happens when reflective groups of teachers examine their classroom teaching with the support of a literacy coach. Although it is certainly true that there are tensions and obstacles in literacy coaching, this book presents a positive approach to literacy coaching and explores both the possibilities for teacher development and the potential for student learning.

There are multiple knowledge bases surrounding effective literacy coaching: adult learning, teacher reflection, literacy development, instructional techniques, classroom assessments, teacher resistance, and collaborative leadership, to name a few. There are entire published books about each of these aspects. However, this book is focused on classroom interactions in which literacy coaches collaborate with teachers and students to find ways to adapt instruction to improve student learning. I use *adapting, modifying,* and *adjusting instruction* to mean the way teachers revise procedures during instruction while maintaining fidelity to their original procedure. *Instructional changes* refer to situations in which teachers change their instructional technique to another form of instruction.

Text Organization

Literacy Coaching: Learning to Collaborate includes five chapters and an instructional techniques section. It focuses on the ways that literacy coaches work with teachers and their students in the classroom.

Chapter 1 explains the role of the school learning community in sustaining literacy coaching. The principal and the literacy coach work together to promote learning throughout the school. Within the classrooms, literacy coaches, teachers, and students form interdependent relationships.

Chapter 2 explains collaboration and collaborative groups. Literacy coaching is a collaborative interaction that supports both teachers' and students' learning, and an understanding of effective collaboration techniques is critically important.

Chapter 3 describes the cycle of literacy coaching and the multiple decisions that teachers make before, during, and after a literacy lesson. During the cycle of preconference, instructional event, and postconference, literacy coaches use various approaches to support teachers as they improve their instructional procedures.

Chapter 4 uses a gradual release model for literacy coaching to explain the different levels of support that literacy coaches can use as they work with teachers. It explains coaching through modeling, "coaching in the zone," and coaching for independence.

Chapter 5 explains ways to observe, analyze, and interpret classroom interactions. The purposes for these actions are to enhance student learning, create instructional adjustments, and extend professional development. These procedures are used throughout the literacy coaching process.

Finally, the instructional techniques section provides detailed procedures for implementing the methods discussed in this book. The instructional techniques are described in a step-by-step fashion so that literacy coaches and teachers can determine at what point instruction was modified to promote student learning. Further, there are suggestions for student and teacher observations when using a specific technique.

Acknowledgments

This text represents a point of view developed over years of coaching teachers as they instructed students in both classrooms and clinics. During that time I have worked with groups of teachers designing coaching models. I am especially thankful for Dana Hardy, Tracy Steigler, Elizabeth Elias, Rene

Beisley, and Melinda Smith, who have collaborated on coaching projects with me. I would also like to thank the clinic supervisors from Spring 2005, who inspired me to think about writing a book.

Special thanks are extended to my reviewers: Jerri L. Foster, Bentonville Public Schools; Claudia Peduzzi, Charlestown Elementary School; and Joan Powell, Whitley County Board of Education.

I have also appreciated the astute judgment of the staff at Pearson Teacher Education and Development, especially to Aurora Martínez for her insightful suggestions for this book and Linda Bishop for her leadership that set the project in motion. I thank production editor Janet Domingo for her untiring efforts to keep the project moving at all times. I am especially thankful for the editorial work of Kathy Smith.

I owe a great deal to each of the teachers who collaboratively discussed their practice and adapted their instruction to improve student learning. Collaboratively analyzing and changing your teaching is hard work. As you engage in coaching activities, please remember the quote from the Velveteen Rabbit, "It doesn't happen all at once. You become. It takes a long time." So it is with becoming an effective literacy coach and a teacher.

Barbara J. Walker

Literacy Coaching

1

Literacy Coaching in a Learning Community

The way that we see things today does not have to be the way we saw them yesterday. That is because the situations, our relationships to them, and we ourselves have changed. . . .

T. K. V. Desikachar

Literacy coaches rally around teachers, supporting their learning and development. Yet, they also challenge teachers to transform their instruction to enhance student learning. They ignite teacher learning by generating queries and challenging accepted wisdom, which encourages teachers to examine their instructional practices and views. As a result, literacy coaches become a catalyst for changing practices, beliefs, and values about literacy and literacy instruction. Thus, literacy coaching is a critical way to advance teachers' knowledge of literacy practices and student learning.

Coaching is certainly not a new concept. The sports arena has always had coaches who supported individuals as they practiced. Coaches like Earl Woods and Hank Haney supported Tiger Woods as he improved his golf swing. These coaches, as well as others, often modeled how to swing a golf club as they said, "Watch how I do it." They might have made suggestions for improvement by supporting what Tiger was doing and demonstrating slight adjustments. Literacy coaching includes many of the same characteristics. It involves collaboration and support for making instructional adjustments that lead to improved student learning.

Literacy coaching in the classroom is a process in which the coaches support teachers as they instruct their students. This is a very personal process that occurs as teachers and literacy coaches work together in the classroom. After teaching, literacy coaches and teachers reflect on student learning and the classroom interactions that produced this learning. They share their perceptions of the teachers' instructional practices and knowledge of literacy instruction. This book is designed to help literacy coaches and teachers work together in classrooms to improve student learning.

Models and Characteristics

There are many models for coaching literacy. Some focus on cognitive aspects, others focus on the collaborative nature of learning, and still others focus on coaching as professional development. This book draws heavily on three models of coaching. In the cognitive coaching model (Costas and Garmston, 2002), coaching is a nonjudgmental process in which a teacher's actions are a result of in-depth thinking and analysis. It focuses on the actions of the individual teacher and the subsequent thinking and analysis by the coach. A three-year study of cognitive coaching showed student scores improved on the Iowa Test of Basic Skills in the coaching schools compared to control schools (Grinder, 1996). The study also showed that teachers engaged in cognitive coaching made fewer recommendations for special education placement.

Another approach, the Boston Collaborative Coaching and Learning project (CCL), has been successful in enabling teachers to use an instructional process in secondary schools (Sturtevant, 2003). In this model, a main characteristic involves active participation by teachers who collaborate with their colleagues. CCL focuses on instructional practice, studies student data, and establishes learning goals within a collaborative group. As a group, the teachers observe a demonstration lesson conducted by the literacy coach, which is followed by a one-hour inquiry period. Next, the teachers use the suggested instructional procedure and analyze their results. Finally, if needed, the coaches offer individual support using one-on-one coaching. Groups of teachers are rotated through these procedures every eight weeks. Neufeld and Roper (2003) evaluated this approach to literacy coaching and found that it improved instructional capacity. They also found that the teachers were more likely to try out new ideas. This Collaborative Coaching and Learning model builds teacher capacity by providing professional development through workshop demonstrations along with individual coaching.

A third model involves coaching as a means for professional development combined with instructional analysis (Lyons & Pinnell, 2001). Key aspects in this model are reflective analysis of teaching and adjusting instruction based on those reflections. The professional development comes when literacy coaches and teachers are debriefing after an instructional event. They engage in deep analysis of instruction, instructional interactions, and student learning. Within this deep analysis, literacy coaches form tentative ideas about the teacher's current understanding and use their insights to focus comments about instruction.

Cognitive coaching, coaching as collaboration, and coaching as instructional analysis are important views of coaching. In this book, literacy coaching involves interactions within the classroom. Like cognitive coaching, literacy coaches and teachers reflect on instruction and student learning in a nonjudgmental way that allows for

Note 1.1 Dana, a Third-Grade Teacher

Dana, a third-grade teacher, used a directed reading-thinking activity (DRTA) in which she asked the students to predict what a story was about by reading the title. Next, she had the students read the story silently. Finally, the students discussed the story (see the Instructional Techniques section). Dana and the literacy coach reflected on the instructional lesson, thinking about student learning. They noticed that Nick seemed to be wildly guessing about story meaning. Dana wondered if Nick's fluency was inhibiting his comprehension, so the literacy coach took Nick aside and asked him to read a paragraph aloud. He orally read the passage with remarkable fluency. Then he retold a few story events, but did not mention the characters or the theme. The literacy coach and Dana decided to adapt the DRTA and add a semantic map (see semantic map in the Instructional Techniques section) to the instructional procedure. They hoped that Nick would contribute to the brainstorming activities, talk about what he knew, and use ideas of other students. It worked! Nick became more engaged in the brainstorming activity and continued this engagement as he was reading. Thus, Nick used the semantic map to activate his prior knowledge to make predictions, relate to the characters, and construct meaning.

deep reflective thinking. As in collaborative coaching, teachers and coaches discuss students' responses in small groups and think of approaches that meet the challenges of their students. Like analytical coaching, the literacy coaches and teachers observe student learning and collect data to analyze student growth and reflect on what occurred. If student learning does not occur, they rethink instruction. Literacy coaching means supporting teachers as they engage students in literacy learning. Thus, in classroom interactions, literacy coaching involves literacy coaches, teachers, and students.

When planning, implementing, and reflecting on instruction, literacy coaches and teachers form a collaborative, decision-making relationship. They talk about student learning and how various instructional approaches and discussions might advance students' learning. Thus, literacy coaches and teachers form the core of instructional change by collaboratively discussing students' learning and interrelating their knowledge about literacy learning. Figure 1.1 demonstrates the collaborative relationship between the literacy coach and the teacher that grows from classroom interactions.

As literacy coaches and teachers discuss the classroom interactions, they reflect on student learning and the instructional situation that produced it. They each share their views of the class-

Figure 1.1

Collaborative Relationship of Classroom Coaching Interactions

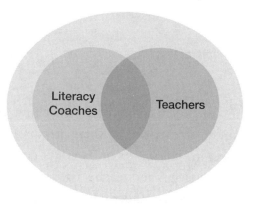

Note 1.2 Dana, a Third-Grade Teacher

Dana discussed her instruction with her colleagues. She explained how the reflective conversations with the literacy coach helped her decide to use a semantic map with the directed reading-thinking activity. Although this was a simple adjustment, it helped Nick understand that story meaning is constructed using what you know and what is in the text. Dana also changed the context by allowing everyone to brainstorm. In this activity, Nick was able to use the ideas of his classmates to prompt his own thinking. The small collaborative group discussed other ways to assist Nick and other students like him.

room interactions and reflect on instruction. The teacher discusses how the students were engaged, while the literacy coach talks about how the teacher skillfully redirected attention to the literacy task rather than focusing on student behavior.

To gather more ideas, literacy coaches discuss the classroom interactions with a small group of teachers with whom they exchange ideas on adapting or augmenting instruction. In these ways, literacy coaches provide frequent and ongoing support for classroom interactions.

A feature of literacy coaching includes forming collaborative groups in which teachers and coaches share their knowledge of student learning and teaching practices and talk about what occurred during instruction. Sometimes, they discuss these reflections in small groups and create a support network. Often, literacy coaches work with several collaborative groups of teachers. These groups

Figure 1.2

Small Collaborative Groups

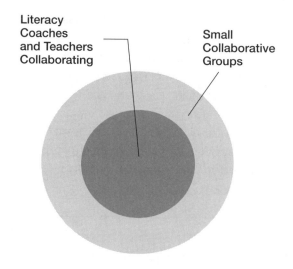

Literacy
Coaches
and Teachers
Collaborating

Small
Collaborative
Groups

form a second layer of collaborative interactions within the school community, as demonstrated in Figure 1.2. As these groups flourish, they form a larger collaborative learning community.

The Learning Community

As groups of teachers and literacy coaches reflect on student learning and discuss those reflections with others, they create a learning community. According to DuFour (2004), a learning community involves a focus on classroom learning and interactions rather than solely on teaching. Thus, teachers and literacy coaches discuss and reflect on student learning and create opportunities for enhanced classroom interactions. In fact, Richardson and Anders (2005) found that as groups of teachers in a school were involved in a learning community, they advanced their understanding of literacy and their students became increasingly literate. Thus, literacy coaches and teachers should take time to sustain thoughtful conversations about literacy and literacy instruction. In the process, they develop relationships that enable them to learn from each other and begin to collaborate on ideas about instruction that will advance student learning. Within a learning community, literacy coaches and teachers discuss issues of instruction and contemplate innovative ways of promoting student learning.

Thus, as teachers and literacy coaches create a context in which they can share their thinking, they establish powerful learning experiences for the entire school community. The learning community involves everyone in the school in discussions about literacy learning. All personnel, including school administrators, become part of the learning community. In fact, principals are of critical importance in learning communities. As school leaders (literacy coaches and principals) and teachers discuss learning, they articulate goals for a positive academic future for students and express a genuine concern for their learning. Principals can develop the broader school community and provide significant support by encouraging teachers to participate in the learning community. As members of the learning community talk with each other, their understanding of literacy and literacy instruction advances.

Literacy Coaches in the Learning Community

Literacy coaches, along with principals, take the lead in sustaining a learning community. They help teachers identify instructional needs and discuss their common vision of improving student learning. Through collaborative discussions, everyone adds to the shared understanding of literacy. The learning community involves everyone in collaborating to improve everyone's learning. It engulfs the total school community. Thus, the final layer in Figure 1.3 surrounds the classroom coaching interactions and the small collaborative groups. The entire figure represents the learning community, with each layer influencing the others. Thus, collaborative and thoughtful conversations move the learning community forward. Within the learning community, literacy coaches help teachers think about their daily teaching and their personal beliefs.

Figure 1.3

The Learning Community

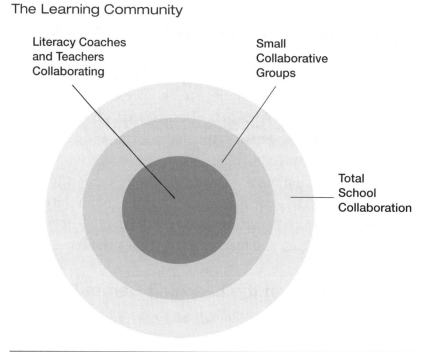

Thus, the literacy coach plays a key role in developing ongoing support for literacy instruction and providing leadership in the learning community.

During classroom interactions, literacy coaches build on the strengths and knowledge that teachers possess. They think about how to develop knowledge about literacy and literacy instruction as they encourage innovative practices. They carefully plan how to create collaborative experiences so the teachers can develop trusting relationships. Finally, they observe classroom teachers instructing students and develop ways to support each teacher's practice. The following sections explain these roles. Although there are certainly other aspects that literacy coaches develop and use as they coach, these are clearly the ones that are paramount.

Knowledge about Literacy and Literacy Instruction

Within the learning community, teachers and literacy coaches develop a commitment to teaching literacy, and in the process they enhance their expertise in literacy instruction. Thus, literacy coaches are an important part of developing expertise within classroom interactions. According to the International Reading Association (2004), literacy coaches need to expand their knowledge of literacy processes and development as well as literacy instructional procedures and ongoing assessment in order to provide the on-the-spot expertise during and after classroom interactions.

Furthermore, there is a knowledge base for literacy that is important for continual teacher development (IRA, 2005). Drawing from several sources (Gambrell, Malloy, & Mazzoni, 2006; Braunger & Lewis, 2005), the following are five elements that are important in literacy instruction.

1. Literacy entails the construction of meaning from various types of materials (novels, textbooks, Internet, etc.) and in various kinds of situations (classroom interactions, report writing, public debates, reading for pleasure, etc.).

2. Engagement and social interactions are keys in becoming literate and developing as a reader and writer.

3. Literacy involves complex thinking as students engage with authentic information and literature.

4. Literacy is a developmental process.

5. Literacy strategies and skills are developed through a variety of literacy opportunities, models, demonstrations, and abundant opportunities for reading and writing.

There are many publications literacy coaches can read to expand their current knowledge about literacy theories and instruction. Often, groups of teachers read or hear about creative instructional procedures or the literacy coach might suggest innovative practices. They begin by talking about these ideas within a collaborative group, with a partner, or with the literacy coach. Literacy coaches follow up by searching for information on the innovation.

Literacy coaches provide information about current theories and research so teachers can discuss the relevant features of a specific teaching practice. Therefore, it is critical that literacy coaches have a solid knowledge base in literacy and literacy instruction so they can thoroughly explain a specific instructional practice.

Knowledge and Use of Collaboration Leading a learning community and discussing teaching in reflective groups require expertise in collaboration. Usually, teachers work in isolation, imple-

Note 1.3 Sixth-Grade Teachers

A group of sixth-grade teachers wanted to develop their students' vocabulary knowledge. In their collaborative group, they described what they knew about vocabulary development. During the week, the literacy coach selected articles on vocabulary development from the *Journal of Adolescent and Adult Literacy* as well as other journals. The literacy coach brought several books to the next group meeting. The teachers and the literacy coach discussed information on vocabulary and selected a book to study for the next couple of weeks.

menting the approved curriculum in their own classrooms. However, collaboration is by definition a social interaction that requires teachers to continually share their thinking and create options for teaching. A shared goal is essential for collaboration to be successful. For literacy coaching in classroom interactions, the shared goal focuses on student learning and instructional practices. Thus, literacy coaching becomes a collaborative problem-solving process.

Teachers count on the literacy coach and other teachers to suggest alternative perspectives to troubling issues and to help them develop insightful solutions. Supportive collaborative interaction is a new way for teachers to learn. Literacy coaches have to learn how to collaborate and then how to guide others to collaborate. Chapter 2 discusses collaboration in more depth.

Supporting Teachers' Practice Literacy coaches support teachers' practice during coaching conversations by observing and

Note 1.4 Jessica, a Second-Grade Teacher

In a second-grade class, Jessica was teaching reading using the *Frog and Toad* series. However, she had six students who were not progressing. She consulted her literacy coach, who listened to each student read a section of *Frog and Toad.* They stopped frequently to sound out words and were reading word by word. The coach and Jessica decided to have the students retell the *Frog and Toad* story. Jessica prompted the students as they retold the story and the literacy coach acted as the scribe. Then, Jessica had the students read their summary aloud. They were able to read their summaries even though they contained difficult story words. However, because the summary was in their own words, they were successful. That day, each student took home a copy of their story to read to their parents.

reinforcing instructional practices and jointly reflecting with teachers. Coaches often support teachers by lending a hand when difficult learning situations arise.

To offer support, literacy coaches think about what teachers know and the language they use to explain their actions. By reflecting on previous interactions with teachers, literacy coaches identify the way a particular teacher talks about his or her practice. Literacy coaches can then think of explanations, and recast them in the teacher's own instructional language. Additionally, coaches should use concrete examples when they support teachers' thinking. They might discuss a teaching interaction by saying, "I noticed how you modeled how to say the word by stretching out the sounds rather than by prompting with another question. That was an effective way to respond." Thus, literacy coaches collaboratively discuss classroom interactions and teachers' practices (see Chapter 3).

Literacy coaches notice students' actions and the way the teachers' instruction enhances their learning. What coaches notice becomes an important part of their conversations with teachers. Using classroom interactions, literacy coaches can support teachers' practices.

Teachers in the Learning Community

Within the learning community, teachers and literacy coaches focus on student learning as their most important goal. The teachers discuss student learning with their coaches, concentrating on instructional adjustments that might improve learning. In a large-scale study of low-performing students, Kennedy (1998) found that when teachers focused on student learning rather than approaches to instruction, they advanced student learning. As they focused on learning, they began to identify the instruction that produced the learning. Thus, teachers learned from analyzing student learning. But they also learned by discussing with other teachers and the literacy coach the factors that promote literacy learning.

Within a learning community, teachers continually develop their expertise. They have opportunities to talk about subject matter, students and learning, and teaching (Wilson & Berne, 1999). Teacher learning involves many aspects, such as previous teaching experiences and beliefs about literacy. However, there are three aspects that are most important to teachers and literacy coaches. First, teachers have many experiences to think about when considering innovative teaching practices. Second, although they often reflect on their instruction, sharing these reflections with other teachers and the literacy coach may be a new experience. Finally, teachers develop their reasons for teaching as they practice. These aspects are expanded on next.

Multiplicity of Experiences When working with teachers to develop their expertise, literacy coaches realize that teachers have a multiplicity of experiences. Many have traveled extensively, raised children, and continued their education. These teachers have accumulated extensive general and specific knowledge about teaching. In fact, after a few years, teachers think about their teaching experiences by recalling specific incidents and children in various learning situations. Thus, they develop some of their expertise by reflecting on real cases from their teaching experience. In this approach to learning, the teachers utilize their experiences as they construct new knowledge about teaching and student learning.

Reflection Effective teachers rethink their instruction. In real life, they shift between being immersed in instruction and stepping back in order to systematically review or reflect on their experiences (Walker, 2008). In fact, reflecting on and discussing those reflections within a learning community helps teachers understand teaching. In order to share their reflections, some teachers keep a journal, whereas others simply keep notes. Discussing reflections about classroom interactions may be a new experience for some teachers, and it can be a powerful experience to observe other teachers reflecting on their students' learning. Thus, the reflective discussion facilitates the way that teachers explain their thinking to others. During reflection and discussion, teachers thoughtfully consider their teaching experiences as well as their assumptions about literacy and literacy instruction.

Practical Reasoning When teachers engage in practical reasoning, they become acutely aware of the unconsciously developed assumptions that guide their practice. As teachers reflect on their practice and grapple with the challenges of their work, they take action. Teachers' actions often appear intuitive. However, in reality, these actions are deeply embedded in experiences, understandings, and interpretations that they have developed to make sense of their practice. As they talk about their practice, teachers verbalize their thinking, making their intuitive actions more apparent. In this way, they intertwine their practice with their reasoning. In collaborative conversations, teachers often compare their reasoning to that of their colleagues. As teachers describe their own teaching experiences, colleagues and literacy coaches can help them refine their practical reasoning.

Interrelationships of Classroom Interactions

The literacy coaching model focuses on literacy coaches, teachers, and students working together to improve classroom learning. Figure 1.4 represents the interconnectedness that occurs as students, teachers, and literacy coaches operate in concert, working toward a common goal. Individual perspectives are shared, but over time, these perspectives overlap as students, teachers, and literacy coaches learn together.

At the core of literacy coaching are the interactions among students, teachers, and literacy coaches. The teacher provides opportunities for the students to discuss literacy learning; the literacy coach provides opportunities for teachers to discuss literacy instruction; and finally, the teacher and the literacy coach

Figure 1.4

The Interrelationships of Classroom Interactions

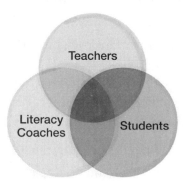

discuss how their understanding and knowledge are expanding. In doing this, everyone develops a common understanding of literacy learning and instruction. All learners' actions influence both learning and specific interactions during instruction. For example, if a teacher adapts instruction, students often respond by using ingenious ways of thinking, thus altering future interactions. The literacy coach tries to capture the learning that occurred by noticing and noting the specific instructional interaction that precipitated this change. Therefore, everyone becomes a literacy informant, revealing how learning evolves as interactions change.

Literacy Coaches and Teachers in the Classroom

Literacy coaches adeptly support teachers as they improve student learning. Further, literacy coaches and teachers depend on each others' observations and perspectives. They connect their perspectives as they discuss literacy learning, student actions, and personal growth. As they take action together, literacy coaches provide support for teachers during instruction. They understand that teachers make appropriate choices for themselves at any given moment. They acknowledge the choice and ask about the student actions that prompted such a choice. Further, they discuss possible alternative procedures during their conversations. Encouraging reflection, the literacy coach might say, "Yes, you can do that, but what are some other choices?" In this way, they encourage teachers to think about options or alternative instructional procedures that could improve student learning.

However, even within this supportive environment, some teachers are stymied and need to actively refocus their efforts. Others are resistant to changing their instruction or classroom interactions. The literacy coach, the principal, and other teachers should try to encourage these teachers to participate within the learning community. To head off teacher resistance, literacy coaches can discuss students' literacy and mentor the teacher by asking questions about classroom interactions. In a conversation with the teacher, they might ask, "What kind of instruction are you using?" or "What specific literacy task are you trying to improve?" By empathetically listening to the responses, literacy coaches can support the teacher's current instruction. They can identify the teacher's strengths and focus him or her on activities that utilize these strengths. (See *The Literacy Coach's Survival Guide* and *Surviving but Not Yet Thriving* by Cathy Toll for further discussion on teacher resistance.)

Students in the Classroom

In the emphasis on teacher change, we often forget about the students and how critical their learning is. In this book, coaching is a process in which literacy coaches and teachers continually analyze their thinking along with that of their students. Students are "no longer docile listeners but they are critical co-investigators in dialogue with the teacher" (Freire, 1970/2005, pp. 80–81). Students are active learners that can contribute to conversations about learning. In fact, as they discuss the content of what they are reading and writing, they indicate both what they already know and what they are learning. The students' learning, discussion, and reflection become a focal point for conversational interactions among the literacy coaches and the teachers. Truly, the innovations and ideas they have are dependent on how the students interact within the classroom context.

Summary

Literacy coaching includes students, teachers, and literacy coaches acting together to advance learning in the classroom. Although the focus of promoting student learning is foremost, teachers and literacy coaches are also learning. Together, teachers and literacy coaches develop their expertise and practices. Even though they are all learning, they are also interdependent on the actions of the others. The classroom interactions bring into play the interrelationships among the literacy coaches, the teachers, and the students. They are integral to the coaching process in the classroom.

2

Coaching and Collaboration

Serious collaboration—teachers engaging in the rigorous mutual examination of teaching and learning—is rare, and where it exists, it is fragile.

Mortan Inger

Collaboration permeates literacy coaching. The literacy coach works toward developing collaborative relationships that lay the groundwork for the learning community, group discussions, and individual conversations. There are many reasons for forming collaborative groups in schools, but the most significant is that collaborative interactions within a learning community improve the learning of both teachers and students (Richardson & Anders, 2005). In fact, research supports the relationship between the existence of a professional learning community and increases in student achievement (McLaughlin & Talbert, 2001).

The literacy coach is instrumental in establishing collaborative relationships and dialogue among groups of teachers. However, collaborative relationships are not easy to develop because teachers are isolated. In fact, Holdzkom (2001) suggests that numerous schools have "intense isolation among teachers, between teachers and administrators, and between parents and teachers" (p. 2). Although teachers often discuss their ideas, it is usually in a cooperative way. They talk about innovative instruction and make suggestions to

Note 2.1 Sixth-Grade Teachers Studying Vocabulary

At the launch of the school year, a group of sixth-grade teachers decided to learn more about vocabulary instruction. The literacy coach posed the question: In what ways can students learn word meanings? The group began generating ideas and focused on the content of vocabulary instruction. At first, the teachers were reluctant to share the ways they taught word meanings during classroom interactions. The literacy coach waited for a response, and finally began to talk about using a graphic organizer (see the Instructional Techniques section). After that, a few teachers explained their vocabulary instruction methods using concrete classroom examples illustrating how they taught word meanings. Each teacher actively listened. The literacy coach commented, "I appreciate the examples you used to clarify your explanations." Thus, the literacy coach and other teachers used positive statements about vocabulary instruction and shared a few experiences. While they were talking, several teachers decided to use graphic organizers in their science teaching. Using this initial process, the literacy coach began to build relationships.

improve student learning. However, no one really has to implement these new ideas.

Collaboration is the inverse process. It is by definition a social interaction in which two or more people work toward a common goal. True collaboration involves teachers jointly discussing ideas and deciding on instructional approaches to use during classroom interactions. In this process, they share their views on literacy instruction and accept other points of view. Establishing a collaborative climate is an evolutionary process. Collaboration in literacy coaching is something individuals come to know and includes the way one thinks about how students learn and how adults work together to support that learning.

Attributes of Collaboration

Literacy coaches collaborate in large groups, small groups, and one-on-one situations. They seldom work alone or in a vacuum. They rely on groups of teachers to share their expertise. In effective coaching situations, teachers and literacy coaches understand and use collaboration in groups by engaging in collaborative discussions. They understand and develop the key attributes (Walker, Scherry, & Gransberry, 2001) that are essential for collaboration: trust, active listening, shared goals, belief in added value, and perspective sharing. These attributes are listed in Table 2.1.

Table 2.1

Attributes of Collaboration

1. Trust
2. Active Listening
3. Shared Goals
4. Belief in Added Value
5. Perspective Sharing

Trust

Within collaborative groups, each interaction builds an environment of mutual trust. Trust building is a process of relationship building that does not occur quickly. Over time and through mutual respect, group members become comfortable moving between giving advice and accepting suggestions from others. When important viewpoints are shared, every teacher and literacy coach keeps the view confidential. The teachers' and the literacy coaches' ability to maintain confidentiality affects the degree to which the group develops trust. One of the cornerstones of collaborative interactions is developing trusting relationships. In these groups, teachers work toward a common goal in an open and honest atmosphere.

Active Listening

During collaborative discussions, everyone listens intently to each speaker's explanations and asks questions to clarify understanding. In order to share understandings, teachers and literacy coaches must believe that others are truly listening to what they are saying. This means that everyone actively listens to the views of each group member as if that person was saying something that increased understanding of the instructional issue at hand.

Shared Goals

An important characteristic of collaboration is that teachers and school leaders understand what the school is trying to do. That is, they have a clear vision and develop shared goals together. A shared vision and subsequent goals unite the learning community around a common purpose. A strong, shared vision focuses awareness on the promise and possibilities of schooling. Both the vision and the goals are constructed within a learning community and collaborative groups. Thus, the common set of goals facilitates taking action

Note 2.2 A Vision for a School

In a small rural school, the teachers and school leaders collaboratively discussed the vision for their school. They came up with
several lofty ideas, but finally jointly decided on the vision that
was captured by the phrase: Leaders, Teachers, and Students
Learning Together. Using this vision, the collaborative groups
generated ideas for goals. Then, the entire school decided on
two shared goals for that year. One was advancing student
learning through adapting instruction. The other was advancing
teachers' learning by collaborating with literacy coaches.

together. Visible actions toward the shared goals create a "spirit of
collaboration and sustain willingness to support the shared goals"
(Holdzkom, 2001, p. 3).

Collaboration Adds Value

At the heart of collaboration are teachers and literacy coaches who
believe that collaboration adds value to the learning community.
Literacy coaches and teachers learn to value all ideas and views that
are put forth. The variety of different viewpoints and experiences
in the learning community adds strength and power to the joint
decisions about shared goals and subsequent mutually developed
teacher actions. Thus, everyone views all members of the learn-

ing community as having equally valuable ideas and actions that contribute to the shared goals. In fact, teachers and school leaders believe that working collaboratively and sharing ideas is a more advantageous way to reach the shared goals. When teachers and literacy coaches share their ideas, the collaborative groups have more possibilities for creating effective literacy instruction.

Perspective Sharing

Teachers and literacy coaches learn to share emerging ideas and perspectives. Sharing views or perspectives requires that individuals state their ideas clearly and concisely. Teachers and literacy coaches use descriptive and understandable language so that everyone can understand their point of view. They often include an example

Note 2.3 Peggy, a Sixth-Grade Teacher

Peggy, a member of the sixth-grade collaborative group study-ing vocabulary, valued reading high-quality literature. As the group discussed vocabulary and shared various techniques, she tried out their suggestions. She used semantic mapping and a graphic organizer called structured overview (see the Instructional Techniques section). She observed her students developing multiple word meaning strategies. By sharing her view and listening to other perspectives, her ideas about vocabulary learning changed.

from their personal life or their classroom teaching that makes their point of view evident. Thus, they share their expertise, knowledge, and beliefs on literacy instruction.

The power of collaboration is that all points of view are valued and shared. As participants "try on" each perspective, they suspend judgment and honestly attempt to understand each teacher's position. As relationships among the teachers grow, they consider each other's insights; this process eventually influences the thinking of all of the teachers. The collaborative group recognizes that within the group process, teachers transform their views. Thus, respect for individual perspectives as growing and changing is essential.

Although groups of teachers have always worked together, they have not had to use each other's ideas. What makes collaboration different is that everyone is committed to a shared goal and so their discussions and actions are directed toward that goal.

Situations for Collaboration

There are many reasons for forming collaborative groups in schools. Sometimes, teachers and other school personnel collaborate within the larger learning community while teachers and literacy coaches collaboratively discuss classroom interactions. Some groups of teachers reflect on classroom instruction, while others discuss their interpretations of professional readings. Still other groups develop, implement, and discuss teacher-research projects to inform their practices. Collaboration occurs in multiple situations throughout the school day.

Collaboration in the Learning Community

Learning communities promote collaborative interactions within the school community at large. According to McLauglin and Talbert (2006), the ability to collaborate is one of the core attributes of schooling. Even though each teacher's development is essential, the whole school's capacity to learn is a collaborative undertaking. Principals often lead this charge by establishing a learning community. Within the learning community (see Figure 2.1), the principal

Figure 2.1

The Learning Community and Literacy Leaders

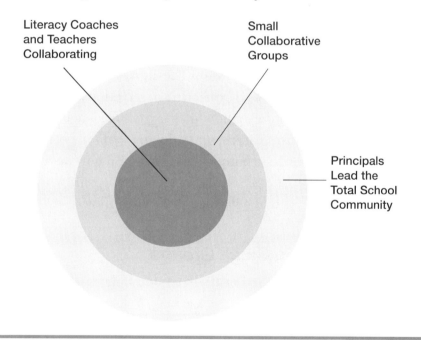

Literacy Coaches
and Teachers
Collaborating

Small
Collaborative
Groups

Principals
Lead the
Total School
Community

involves the total school in collaborative conversations. Then, the principal leads the learning community in developing the school's vision. Literacy coaches and other informal leaders participate in the process and then use the school's vision as a focus for the smaller collaborative groups' shared goals. In fact, another structure of a professional learning community is small collaborative groups that share the school's vision. It is within the smaller collaborative groups that literacy coaches provide the support for the learning community.

Collaboration in Classroom Interactions

In the classroom, the literacy coach and the teacher collaborate on literacy instruction. In their relationship, they share points of view as they work toward a shared goal of increasing student learning within classroom interactions. The collaboration includes the planning and analysis of a specific lesson. The literacy coach and the teacher clarify what happened by sharing observations and reviewing data. By clarifying information, they use precise language to explain their experiences and current thinking. Both the literacy coach and the teacher have unique perspectives on how instruction occurred. By sharing perspectives, they identify and reflect on key instructional elements that advanced student learning.

Collaborations in Small Groups

During small group interactions, collaboration increases teachers' knowledge of practice and literacy learning. In fact, collaboration often involves sharing instructional and personal assumptions about literacy learning. As the teachers learn more about each other, they are willing to share deep-rooted ideas. Small collaborative groups focused on special functions support both the literacy coaches and the teachers learning together.

Reflective Discussion Groups Reflective discussions encourage teachers and literacy coaches to think and talk about literacy and literacy instruction. Often, reflective discussions occur after several teachers have implemented specified instructional procedures. Sometimes a teacher or literacy coach initiates the discussion by asking a question that requires everyone to reflect upon instruction. They might ask: "What did you do that influenced student learning?" or "Were there any surprises?" or "What changes could be made?" As they discuss these questions, teachers and literacy coaches clarify their thoughts and beliefs. During the discussion, literacy coaches listen closely to the teachers' assumptions about literacy learning. The teachers and the literacy coaches begin to change their beliefs. Reflecting on their developing views of literacy learning leads the way for teachers to reconsider not only their

Box 2.1

Reflective Discussion Groups

Reflective Discussion Groups focus on implemented instructional techniques and student responses. As teachers and literacy coaches discuss teachers' actions, they clarify their beliefs about literacy learning.

instructional methods but also their beliefs about teaching. In this way, both the teachers and the coaches advance their understanding of literacy instruction.

Study Groups Study groups often emerge out of the learning community and are organized around a particular theme or topic. The literacy coach and teachers collaboratively select a topic like struggling readers, strategy instruction, or writing. These groups have typically revolved around discussing professional journal articles or books related to a chosen topic. Having everyone read the same article or professional book facilitates the development of a common language around the theme selected. However, creating a study group that supports dialogue and teacher talk requires a deep commitment (Birchak, Connor, Crawford, Kahn, Kaser, Turner, & Short, 1998). As groups study concepts, their language becomes more sophisticated as their ideas grow. In study group situations, the literacy coach steers the collaborative interactions, helping teachers share their perspectives. During this process, they consider innovative ideas about instruction.

Box 2.2

Study Groups

> Study groups focus on a group-selected theme and professional reading. The group reads, interprets, and discusses the theme in reference to the professional reading.

Note 2.4 Fluency Study Group

A group of second-grade teachers wanted to focus on fluency. The teachers had a well–developed knowledge about word identification strategies, but wanted to know more about fluent reading with comprehension. Maria, the literacy coach, gave book talks on several professional books dealing with fluency instruction. The teachers decided to read and discuss *The Fluent Reader* (Rasinski, 2003). As the teachers read the book, they began to implement suggested practices. In the study groups, they discussed what fluent reading was and ways to support it. Their talk changed from "Where are we going tonight for dinner?" to "What kinds of phrasing and intonation are your students using as they read poetry?" In this way, they held each other accountable for making instructional changes during their classroom interactions.

Teacher-Research Groups In teacher-research groups, a group of teachers who are committed to improving their practice study innovative ideas together. During the collaborative discussion, the teacher-research group decides on a teaching issue they want to study. First, they study information about the instructional procedure. Second, they establish the classroom procedures for instruction and decide on what data to collect both before and after instruction. Third, they reflect on what occurred and collect data.

Table 2.2

Teacher Research Procedures

1. Select an instructional practice.

2. Study the practice.

3. Establish classroom procedures.

4. Decide on what data to collect.

5. Implement procedures.

6. Reflect on instruction.

7. Analyze data.

8. Share outcomes with teacher-research group.

Finally, they analyze the data and share the outcomes in a collaborative discussion about the research project.

Before the teacher-research begins, the literacy coach and the teachers gather information about the procedure and then collaboratively discuss how to implement the procedure, the rationale for using it, and its theoretical assumptions. Then in a workshop usually before or after school, the literacy coach demonstrates using the instructional practice and the teachers discuss the procedure.

The collaborative discussions that occur in the teacher-research groups support teachers' learning. Every teacher shares significant aspects of his or her teaching, as well as the student learning that occurred. As the groups continue, they begin to share how their

Note 2.5 Teacher-Research Group

A group of kindergarten and first-grade teachers formed a teacher-research group to learn about the instructional practice of Interactive Writing (see the Instructional Techniques section). The teachers met weekly for an hour during their joint planning time right after lunch. Wanda, a kindergarten teacher, believed that writing instruction didn't start until late in first grade. It certainly was not her responsibility. Despite Wanda's views, the teacher-research group decided to implement interactive writing. The others convinced Wanda to try it out. After instruction, teachers reviewed and analyzed their observations and the writing samples. They reflected on how the instruction improved student learning and shared those reflections within the teacher-research group. Wanda explained her students' writing performance as she showed writing samples. After a couple of weeks, however, Wanda began discussing her beliefs and expectations about young children's writing. Wanda learned that most kindergarten children could write sentences. Thus, she changed her views about the amount and kind of writing kindergarten and first-grade children can do.

practice is changing as a result of the research they are doing. They often discuss the changes they made as they taught and how those changes influenced both student learning and their own thinking.

Summary

Individuals who are willing to work together in an open and honest atmosphere are integral to collaboration. They share their knowledge about literacy and literacy instruction and discuss how their beliefs influence their instruction. These collaborative interactions help teachers reflect on student learning and instructional procedures in light of their changing beliefs.

The Cycle of Literacy Coaching

In three words I can sum up everything I've learned about life: it goes on.

Robert Frost

Like life, learning goes on. Literacy coaching is a dynamic process in which all participants advance their understanding. Throughout the coaching cycle, literacy coaches and teachers maintain a strong desire to meet the challenges that arise during classroom interactions. Before the cycle begins and after the cycle is complete, the literacy coach and the teachers discuss classroom interactions within a reflective group. Thus, literacy coaches are open to ideas that support the learning of both teachers and students.

This chapter outlines the cycle of literacy coaching. Teachers and literacy coaches are involved in a cycle of coaching that comprises a preconference, an instructional event, and a postconference. The cycle of coaching contains multiple interrelated aspects that enhance everyone's learning. As it nears completion, a new cycle begins, creating a continuous process of learning and development. Students become literate and take control of their learning; teachers become more flexible, readily adapting instruction; and literacy coaches become adept at leading collaborative interactions and promoting reflective thinking.

Note 3.1 Gail, the Literacy Coach

Gail, the literacy coach at an elementary school, visited several classrooms and participated in team meetings. She also observed classroom literacy interactions. Several of the second- and third-grade teachers had a delightful short conversation about retelling. They had read about retelling and discussed this aspect of reading comprehension in their study group.

Section 1
Getting Started

Literacy coaching during classroom interactions commences within collaborative groups that aspire to enhance their practice. Thus, the foundation of this process is a small reflective group that shares literacy knowledge and designs innovative teaching methods. Before the coaching cycle begins, literacy coaches talk with groups of teachers and gain their respect by actively listening as they describe their classroom interactions. Throughout the process, coaching conversations between teachers and literacy coaches unite each aspect of the cycle. In these conversations, the literacy coaches and teachers discuss various ways to develop engaging learning situations. In this way, they contribute to the learning community and meet the challenges that teachers and students face.

Getting to Know Each Other

As literacy coaches visit teachers' classrooms, they establish themselves as part of the classroom environment. The students and the
teacher become accustomed to the coach's presence in the classroom.
During this "getting to know each other" stage, the literacy coach and
the teacher casually brainstorm ways to improve student learning.

Initial Perceptions of Teachers   As literacy coaches get to
know the teachers they work with, they form their initial perceptions of them (Lyons & Pinnell, 2001). When teachers discuss their
instructional practice with literacy coaches, the coaches listen and
reflect on the following questions:

> What does the teacher say about students?
>
> How does the teacher describe student literacy actions?
>
> What are the teacher's strengths?
>
> What are the teacher's challenges?
>
> What does the teacher need to work on?
>
> What kind of observations does the teacher make?
>
> How does the teacher analyze student work?

These reflections help coaches form perceptions about how teachers think about their expertise. These perceptions will continue to
be refined throughout the coaching experience as new insights are
gained.

Setting the Tone of Collaboration   Coaching interactions
often begin in small collaborative groups, and teachers may be

hesitant to participate in one-to-one conversations with literacy coaches. Realizing this, literacy coaches focus on building relationships of trust as they converse about instructional practices and student learning. They actively listen to teachers as they describe their practice, accepting all information without judging it. They become participants in classrooms and talk freely with both students and teachers. Building on these relationships, teachers and coaches can then establish joint goals for instruction.

Coaching Conversations

Using student learning as a common goal, literacy coaches and teachers discuss various avenues for developing engaging learning situations. These conversations do not involve a discrete instructional event in which the literacy coach is present, but rather are follow-up exchanges about classroom interactions (Lyons & Pinnell, 2001). Sometimes, these conversations occur in hallways or in the teachers' lounge.

Conversations about Instructional Practices Most teachers are comfortable talking about their current practices. So literacy coaches can casually ask about what they do in their classrooms. Sometimes teachers talk about the content they are teaching, but they may also talk about how to form small group discussions about content. Other teachers may be curious about how to use writing to support their content area instruction.

Conversations about Student Learning In these conversations, literacy coaches can develop relationships with the teachers. From brief visitations and conversations, literacy coaches and teachers begin discussing students and their learning in the classroom. In these discussions, teachers often reveal their perspectives on instructional procedures and student learning. These casual conversations are an important part of literacy coaching, and they will continue throughout the coaching process. Reflecting on the conversations, literacy coaches may form tentative ideas about teaching practices. Coaches use their interpretation of teachers' actions to formulate ways of talking with them using the teachers' language patterns and knowledge base.

Section 2
The Literacy Coaching Cycle

The literacy coaching cycle involves three broad phases: a preconference, an instructional event, and a postconference. The cycle of literacy coaching involves layers of actions that occur as teachers and literacy coaches analyze and reflect on student learning (Costas & Garmston, 2002; Lyons & Pinnell, 2001). Literacy coaches, teachers, and students are involved in all aspects of the cycle of literacy coaching. The phases occur in a cyclic pattern, as illustrated in Figure 3.1.

During the preconference stage, literacy coaches and teachers discuss student learning. During instruction, the teachers focus on students and ask them about their learning. Within the instructional event, literacy coaches observe students' learning and the teacher's actions that produced it. Afterward, teachers and literacy coaches jointly discuss their perceptions as well as possible alternatives that have a high probability of increasing student learning.

Figure 3.1

The Cycle of Literacy Coaching

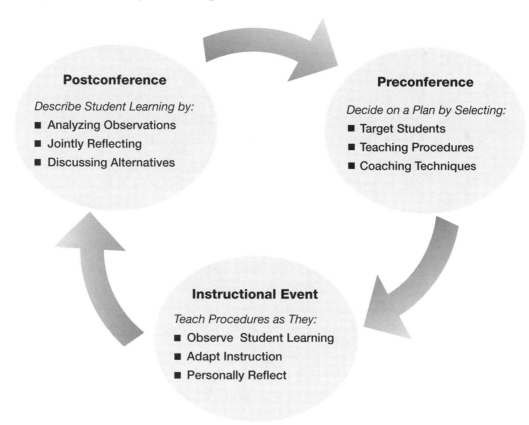

Thus, the preconference, the instructional event, and the postconference involve a cyclical process. These phases are elaborated on in
the following discussion.

Preconference

After a few weeks, coaches and teachers arrange to meet for a pre-conference that occurs before a formal observation of the class. In this conference, they discuss current student learning, review any student work that has been collected previously, and collaboratively plan ways to increase student learning. The preconference offers opportunities for the literacy coach to continue to build a trusting relationship with a teacher. Thus, the literacy coach listens closely, lets the teacher take the lead in explaining the thinking behind instructional plans, and empathizes with the teacher's challenges.

During the preconference, the literacy coach and the teacher discuss the kinds of literacy acts that are important, such as using background knowledge appropriately, monitoring understanding, and summarizing and discussing what has been read. Again, teachers take the lead and describe what they are interested in learning or understanding. The coach listens to the teachers as they add some ideas and agree to keep an eye on aspects that are jointly considered important. Teachers, then, become participant observers who teach and observe at the same time. Observing student learning is a difficult task if it is done while teaching. Thus, the literacy coach and the teacher select specific students for focused observations.

Selecting Target Students   During this preconference, teachers and literacy coaches discuss various students in the classroom and their subsequent approaches to learning. Together, they select target students and identify learning challenges and patterns. Sometimes, teachers select several students to observe instead of a whole class. Many times, these students represent a range of achievement; at other times, teachers focus on below-level readers.

Note 3.2 A Group of Third-Grade Teachers

Gail and a small group of third-grade teachers were implementing the retelling technique (see the Instructional Techniques Section) that was suggested during the study group. Andrea, Juan, and Tanya briefly taught some elements of story structure (setting, including characters, problem events, and resolution). Then they had the students retell the story to a partner as the teachers moved around the classroom. As they walked around, they focused on three students (their target students) who had difficulty with comprehension.

Selecting Instructional Procedures During the preconference, the teachers and literacy coaches decide on instructional procedures that might improve literacy. They think about what the learners can do and what they need to know. Then, they think about several instructional practices that might advance these students' learning. In other words, literacy coaches and teachers review both the students' literacy patterns and the teacher's instructional practice to select suitable instructional procedures for them.

When coaching, the discussion of specific instructional techniques helps teachers mentally run through how to teach the lesson. During the discussion, literacy coaches put forward opportunities and scenarios that would lend themselves to adjustments that might enhance student learning.

Note 3.3 Gail and the Third-Grade Teachers

After working with story retelling, Andrea and her colleagues realized that their students did not understand how to retell a story. They talked about this issue with Gail, the literacy coach. After they recounted that during second grade the teachers did not work on comprehension and the students predominantly answered the teachers' literal questions, Gail and the teachers considered alternative teaching procedures. As a group, they selected another similar instructional procedure, the story map (see the Instructional Techniques section).

Selecting Coaching Procedures When teachers and their literacy coach make instructional decisions, they decide how the literacy coach will support their instruction. The literacy coach can support instruction in different ways (see Chapter 4).

Demonstrations If the teacher is unfamiliar with the approach, the coach can offer to model a lesson. The teacher watches the teaching actions of the literacy coach, and observes the students as they respond to the lesson.

Collaborative Teaching If the teacher has tried the procedure, but is still very uncomfortable with the approach, the literacy coach teaches alongside of the teacher. They plan together, sharing ideas about which aspects of the lesson they will teach. For example, the teacher may demonstrate a science activity while the coach writes students' observations on the chalkboard.

Ongoing Support If the teacher is somewhat comfortable with the approach, the literacy coach stands by, ready to assist the teacher with troublesome spots. During the instructional event, the literacy coach stands ready to phase in to support the teacher's actions. The coach also knows when to phase out to let the teacher independently teach the lesson.

Observation If the teacher is comfortable with the procedure, the literacy coach observes the classroom interactions, watching the students' interactions and focusing on the target students as well as the teacher's actions. These observations, then, inform the teacher's practice, including developing modifications to improve the learning of challenging students.

Note 3.4 Gail Coaches Teachers on Story Mapping

In the small group, Gail, the literacy coach, did a quick workshop on story mapping by demonstrating it and discussing it with the group. As they discussed the story map, Andrea and Juan realized that they had taught this procedure, so they decided to teach story mapping without any support. They asked Gail, the literacy coach, to observe. Tanya, however, was less sure of how to implement the story map and needed the literacy coach to collaboratively teach using the story map.

Workshops   Sometimes, teachers want to experience an instructional technique firsthand. In these situations, the literacy coach prepares a lesson and teaches the teachers. Then, the teachers collaboratively describe the instructional technique and discuss how they would use it during their literacy instruction.

As literacy coaches and teachers select coaching techniques, they discuss the teachers' knowledge about the particular technique and the kind of support the teachers want. Some teachers will have had experiences that assist them in understanding and using the instructional procedure without a demonstration lesson. Literacy coaches stand nearby, observing both instruction and student learning, and are open to suggestions and willing to modify their support.

Selecting What to Observe   During the preconference, the literacy coaches and the teachers also decide on what to observe or monitor during the lesson (see Chapter 5 for ideas). The teachers observe student interactions and literacy coaches observe both the teacher's actions and the students' interactions.

Note 3.5 Collecting Story Maps

Andrea, Juan, and Tanya discussed what they wanted to know about their students. Many ideas were shared. The group decided to observe how engaged in story mapping the students were and to collect the story maps to help their analysis.

Teacher Actions Literacy coaches observe the teacher's actions, looking for high engagement in the literacy activities. The literacy coaches note how the teacher keeps the students engaged. Watching the teacher explain literacy learning through modeling and scaffolding gives the coaches insights into the teacher's effectiveness.

Student Actions Teachers and literacy coaches watch students during classroom interactions. Students actively participate in class discussions, revising their understanding while discussing. Students are also critical and reflective thinkers; thus, both teachers and literacy coaches ask them to explain their thinking. In these situations, students justify their interpretations by referring to the text and using their own reasoning to explain their thinking.

Selecting Student Work As teachers watch students, they review their work. The literacy coaches and the teachers decide if they want to collect student work to add to their observations.

Finally, literacy coaches and teachers are ready to begin instruction. They have located a problem in student learning, instructional procedures, or students to watch, and have determined what to observe and the coaching procedure. The next phase of the cycle of literacy coaching involves teachers teaching, students learning, and literacy coaches offering support.

Instructional Event

Within the instructional event, teachers implement the specified procedures while the literacy coaches support their teaching. When implementing a modified or new instructional procedure, the literacy coaches need to have developed a working relationship with the teacher and students. The teachers continue with their everyday routines except for implementing the selected instructional procedures, which keeps classroom interactions normal.

Conversations with Students   After the instructional event, teachers ask students about their learning. They could also ask what they liked about the lesson and if they felt comfortable during the lesson. In addition, teachers might ask about new information or ideas students learned and what they already knew before the lesson. Effective teachers know that students are excellent informants. Interviewing or talking with students about their literacy learning helps teachers reflect on what was happening during the lesson.

The Literacy Coaches' Observation Process   While literacy coaches continue to observe the classroom interactions and student

Note 3.6 Gail and Tanya Collaboratively Teach

Gail, the literacy coach, and Tanya were collaboratively teaching the story mapping technique. Gail often phased in to support Tanya and phased out to let Tanya teach on her own. The procedure was going great except that Tanya had one student who could not fill out the story map. Gail phased in to explicitly explain the story map. Tanya watched how she explained and explicitly modeled the steps for filling out the story map. Then, Gail supported and scaffolded the student's learning.

Note 3.7 Kamal

Gail, the coach, and Andrea observed that Kamal could fill out the setting and character, but included only a brief mention of the problem and had only one event. Together, they discussed their observations. Gail suggested that having the students work in small heterogeneous groups would provide Kamal with several models to follow as he filled out the story map.

learning, they collect observational data and later analyze it for patterns of student learning. They also keep notes on the instructional event by specifically noting student interactions and engagements (see Chapter 5). Literacy coaches also watch how the teachers implement and adjust the instructional procedures.

The Teachers' Observation Process Immediately after the lesson, teachers jot down observations about the instructional event. Later, teachers analyze their jottings, the students' work, and their perceptions about the instructional procedures. Thus, they analyze their instruction and the resulting student learning in light of their observations and reflections.

Personal Reflection Before the postconference, literacy coaches and teachers individually reflect on and analyze the instructional event and organize their thinking. The passage of time (at least

Note 3.8 Evaluating Story Maps

All three teachers decided to collect the story maps for further analysis and discussion in the small reflective group. They discussed what was important to include on the story map, constructed a rubric, and then selected the three story maps to demonstrate levels of performance (see Chapter 5 for a retelling rubric).

a day and no more than two days) before joint reflection helps literacy coaches and teachers contemplate what transpired. They think about the students' responses, including what the students said or did to indicate that they were learning. Individually, they mentally replay scenes from the lesson. In envisioning the instructional event, they also think about teachers' actions that promoted student learning. As teachers engage in instruction, they adapt their original plan in an effort to advance student literacy strategies.

As they think about the instructional event, literacy coaches and teachers reflect about how to make their observations understandable. In fact, literacy coaches often need time to figure out how to use the concepts that the teachers understand and the language they use to describe them. Literacy coaches recast their observations using the teachers' language and perspectives. Building on the teachers' personal assumptions, literacy coaches interact with the teachers discussing the instructional event.

Postconference

After individual reflection, literacy coaches and teachers collaboratively discuss the instructional event. Reflective discussion is a critical aspect of literacy coaching and professional development. The literacy coaches and the teachers begin by sharing their overall perceptions of the instructional event. When they engage in the postconference, they reflect on the information collected and discuss specific aspects of student learning.

Next, literacy coaches and teachers engage in thoughtful discussions about the teachers' actions that furthered student learning. They spend time sharing observational examples of what occurred, analyzing how the instructional technique worked or did not work, and thinking of next steps. Thus, literacy coaches sustain the teachers' reflective analysis about student learning and the instructional procedures that developed it.

Reflecting on Instructional Adjustments
Although the conversation can get off track, literacy coaches and teachers redirect their discussion to focus on student and teacher learning. This continuous refocusing helps teachers refine both their thinking and their reflective analysis. Thus, literacy coaches and the classroom teachers collaborate to explain what instructional adjustments would further enhance the students' engagement and subsequent learning. With the literacy coaches, the teachers reflect on their reasoning and formal theories about literacy learning.

Describing Reasoning in a One-on-One Conversation
Teachers can begin by explaining their practical reasoning to the literacy coaches. The literacy coaches and teachers

compare their perspectives to those of their colleagues, casually talking about their thinking. In this situation, teachers and literacy coaches can reconsider their thinking privately within a trusting relationship. They are able to reflect on instruction and their changing views of literacy learning.

Section 3
After the Coaching Cycle

After the coaching cycle ends, the teachers continue to discuss their instruction and literacy learning. They examine what happened, using classroom examples to elaborate how they made instructional adjustments.

Small Group Reflection

Sometimes, teachers continue to discuss their instruction and their students in the small reflective group. In fact, they share specific and personal views about how instructional modifications increased learning. This discussion supports teachers as they rethink their personal views about literacy and literacy learning. Within the group, the teachers share their fresh understanding about the recent instructional procedures they used.

Reflecting on Practical Reasoning Within the small collaborative group, literacy coaches encourage teachers to examine the beliefs underlying their actions. Using specific instructional examples can facilitate teachers' thinking. They can use the examples to concretely analyze their thinking about a specific instructional

Note 3.9 Reflecting within the Small Group

Andrea, Juan, and Tanya met one afternoon to discuss and compare their outcomes with Gail, the literacy coach. In the small reflective group, they described the reading strategies of their students, the progress they made, and their personal thinking about literacy. Andrea talked about how she thought retelling was a natural rather than a learned strategy. Juan responded that Joseph, a third grader, did not have a clue about retelling what he read. But now, Joseph was retelling stories fairly well. Gail discussed the changing views of Andrea, Juan, and Tanya, and they all agreed that retelling can improve with instruction.

event. Through each discussion, the literacy coach and the teachers modify and clarify their perspectives on literacy learning.

Reflecting on Formal Theories Likewise, literacy coaches help teachers elaborate on their practical reasoning using recognized literacy theories as a lens through which to consider their actions and beliefs. The literacy coach shares with the teachers the recognized theories that support their actions. These discussions provide diverse perspectives on their teaching actions.

Thus, the small, reflective group leads the professional development of teachers as they discuss their thinking in a collaborative group.

Reflecting within the Learning Community Teachers are proud of their professional development and share their successes in small groups, but they also share their successes within the larger learning community. Individually, they talk with their friends and fellow teachers, explaining their development. Some teachers even discuss their growth and their students' learning with their principals. Sometimes principals ask these teachers to present their instructional technique and its implementation during faculty meetings. The teachers also share their experiences with their book study group. Thus, teachers and literacy coaches share their most up-to-date understandings with the wider school community.

Continuing a Coaching Cycle Literacy coaches spend between 6 and 8 weeks with various teachers in order to bring about changes in their thinking about, planning, and adapting of instruction. So, if a group of teachers finishes before the end of the 6-week time frame, they continue the cyclic process and select a different instructional practice before the end of their time with the literacy coach. The literacy coach is already familiar with the classroom interactions, the students, and the teachers, so little time is spent during the "Getting to Know Each Other" aspect of coaching. However, coaching conversations continue on an individual basis. After the 6 to 8 weeks, literacy coaches move on to a different group of teachers.

A New Cycle of Literacy Coaching A new cycle of literacy coaching begins in various ways; however, it often arises out of discussions in the small reflective group or the larger book study group. The new coaching cycle can include the same teachers or another cohort of teachers. In their reflection, literacy coaches and teachers come up with various ways that could advance student learning. In this way, they begin the cycle anew. During the preconference, the literacy coach and teacher finalize the selection of an instructional procedure to improve student learning. The instructional event and postconference continue in the same way as the previous cycle.

Summary

The cycle of literacy coaching engages coaches and teachers as they plan, observe, and analyze instruction. Throughout the process, the coaching conversations become the glue that connects each aspect of the cycle. The literacy coaching cycle consists of a preconference, an instructional event, and a postconference. The backbone of the process is a small reflective group that shares observations and promotes reflection about instruction. As each cycle is near completion, a new cycle begins, creating a continuous process of learning and development.

4

The Gradual Release Model of Classroom Coaching

R eason does not work instinctively, but requires trial, practice, and instruction in order to gradually progress from one level of insight to another.

Immanuel Kant

Literacy coaches support teacher reasoning by probing teachers' reflections on classroom interactions. Teachers try out new instructional techniques, modifying them while they teach. Then, they rethink their instruction and the students' responses. In their reflections, they develop their reasons for teaching, which gradually strengthens their literacy knowledge. There are various approaches that encourage teachers to reflect on their instructional practices and their reasoning. Some coaches use an inquiry approach for professional development and literacy coaching (Lyons & Pinnell, 2001; Rosemary, Roskos & Landreth, 2007). Others use collaborative groups that engage in responsive interactions (Dozier, 2006). Some approaches are focused on specific instructional procedures that are demonstrated in a workshop format (Neufeld & Roper, 2003). After the demonstration, the teachers implement the practice in their classrooms. Other approaches use demonstration and modeling within classroom interactions, followed by supporting teachers' actions and reflecting on practice (Walker, 2008). In this book, the gradual release of classroom coaching model is patterned after the gradual release of responsibility model developed for teacher-student interactions by Pearson and Gallagher in 1983. This dynamic instructional procedure for teaching comprehension progresses from explicit modeling to guided practice to fostering students' independent learning. This model also can be used in coaching.

Using this model for coaching is slightly different. The teachers always have the responsibility to teach, but they do not continuously seek out ways to improve their practice. Thus, literacy coaches provide direct support and develop collaborative interactions in the classroom. Then, literacy coaches release their guided classroom support so that teachers seek out professional conversations and development on their own. Therefore, the model becomes the gradual release of classroom coaching. As in the Pearson and Gallagher model (1983), there is a gradual release of support rather than simply modeling and leaving teachers alone as they practice.

The format suggested for literacy coaches in this book is to gradually withdraw support. Literacy coaches model or demonstrate teaching procedures within the classroom, followed by supporting teachers as they implement the new procedures. Then, they build teacher independence by encouraging them to reflect on their practice both alone and with a reflective group. This process is depicted in Figure 4.1.

In this process, coaches model an instructional practice in the classroom, and teachers watch the coaches interact with their students. When the instructional practices have become more familiar to the teachers, the literacy coaches stand nearby to offer support as the teachers use the procedure. This "coaching in the zone" relies on literacy coaches supporting teachers as they guide students'

Figure 4.1

The Gradual Release of Classroom Coaching Model

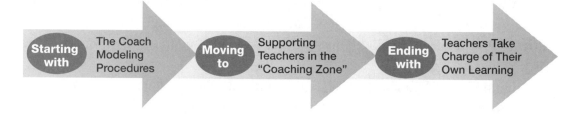

literacy learning. When possible, literacy coaches withdraw from the instructional situation. Thus, the coaches fade out their support for instruction, allowing teachers to proceed independently. This approach can help teachers take control of their instructional practices, which positively impacts both their teaching and student learning. The gradual release of classroom coaching model moves through modeling to coaching in the zone, and then to coaching for independence.

Coaching through Modeling

Literacy coaches demonstrate specified practices as they explain the procedures within classroom interactions. Often teachers need to see "instruction in action" in order to conceptualize the instructional practice.

While literacy coaches model a lesson, teachers observe classroom interactions, focusing on which teacher actions furthered

Note 4.1 A Literacy Studies Class

Karen, the middle-school literacy coach, was discussing Jeremy's literacy learning with Fran, a literacy studies class teacher. Fran recounted that when Jeremy was asked his opinion about a piece of literature, he often responded "I don't know," made a joke, or simply did not respond; therefore, he did not build his comprehension strategies. Karen suggested using a "Think-Aloud" approach with a small group of students. Fran had read about this technique but was uncertain about how to implement it. Because Fran had never used the technique, Karen agreed to model it. Karen taught the "Think Aloud" procedure while Fran observed her students. Karen had to modify her instruction several times, explaining and demonstrating how to revise understanding. After the demonstration lesson, Karen and Fran collaboratively talked about how the students responded.

student learning. In modeling instruction, literacy coaches provide teachers with an example of how to implement the instructional procedure and also demonstrate how to modify instruction to foster student learning. In a large-scale coaching study, researchers found that instructional modeling was an effective means of fostering teacher learning (Poglinco, Bach, Hovde, Rosenblum, Saunders, & Supovitz, 2003). They also found that "seeing the coach demonstrate in the classroom had an important effect on how teachers subsequently modified their practice . . ." (p. 21). Thus, when coaches model a technique, teachers change their instructional practices more readily. As coaches model instructional practices, they demonstrate how to modify their original plan and keep track of their adjustments. This helps teachers not only learn an instructional practice but also understand how to adapt it. A critical aspect of literacy coaching is demonstrating instructional practices and the modifications that increase student learning.

Too often, modeling ends the coaching experience because teachers want to move directly to instructing on their own. However, highly skilled coaches stay in the classroom, observing students' actions and supporting teachers as they implement the specified instructional procedures. At this time, coaches begin challenging teachers to reconsider their personal assumptions.

Coaching in the Zone

In the second phase of the gradual release of classroom coaching model, literacy coaches support teachers as they guide students to increasingly successful literacy experiences. The guided practice continues for several lessons as the literacy coach supports the specified instructional practice. This phase is called "Coaching in the Zone." The "zone" refers to Vygotsky's concept of the *zone of proximal development*, which he defined as the "distance between the actual developmental level as determined by independent problem solving and the level of potential development as determined through problem solving . . . in collaboration with more capable peers" (Vygotsky, 1978, p. 86).

Note 4.2 Fran Teaches "Think Aloud"

Fran and Karen jointly planned the next lesson. Fran decided to conduct the think-aloud lesson with Karen nearby to support her actions. Karen stood near the front of the room so she could phase in when Fran was confused by student responses. When Karen phased in, she modeled her own thinking rather than asking questions. She immediately phased out to let Fran model her own thinking. The rest of the session, Fran waited for a student response. When students did not respond, she modeled her thinking rather than asking a direct question.

In this zone, an individual could learn tasks that he or she normally could not perform independently with support from others. Therefore, when literacy coaches are "coaching in the zone," they offer support to teachers as they instruct a lesson. Their support may include collaborative teaching, supporting teachers' adaptations, or simply phasing in to support the teachers' instruction. The literacy coach uses these support strategies as teachers adjust instruction to meet the students' challenges.

Collaborative Teaching

Literacy coaches can collaboratively teach as the teacher implements instruction. In this way, the literacy coach and the teacher jointly plan and deliver a specified lesson. In collaborative teaching, the teacher implements the suggested practice while the coach assists when needed. Thus, the students see two teachers combining their personal knowledge and expertise. As the teacher moves around the room, chatting with the students about their work, the teacher also talks with the literacy coach. The students see how individuals can help each other understand information.

Supporting by Asking Questions

Sometimes, teachers feel comfortable with their instructional procedures, but are concerned about supporting all students' learning. During an instructional lesson, the literacy coach and the teacher support students' learning by asking questions like those found in Table 4.1.

Other times, the literacy coach or the teacher enter the classroom interactions by asking open-ended questions to help students rethink their understanding (see Table 4.2).

Thus, during classroom interactions, the literacy coach phases in to interject questions and comments that expand the students' thinking. (See *Choice Words* by Peter Johnston for more ideas.)

Table 4.1

Examples of Questions Used During and After Reading

- Have you ever had that kind of experience?
- Can you tell me more about the characters?
- Can you tell me about the important information?
- Can you point to something in the text that makes you think that?

Table 4.2

Open-ended Questions

- How did you figure that out?
- What made you think that?
- Does anyone want to say something more?

Supporting by Prompting

Another way to support understanding is to give students prompts when they stumble as they are reading aloud. When supporting young readers, literacy coaches and teachers can indicate that something did not make sense when students read orally. They prompt students to review what they read. Thus, teachers and coaches may say, "Rethink what you read." Then, they might add other prompts such as "What was the story about?" or "You said 'skate.' Does that make sense in a story about swimming?"

Support for Modifying Instruction

Teachers sometimes want support in modifying instruction for certain students. In these situations, literacy coaches move around the room, helping and observing students, making notes, and monitoring how the target students are learning. As the teacher is instructing, the literacy coach may observe an opportunity to modify instruction and step in to show the teacher how to orchestrate an adaptation to increase student learning.

In this way, literacy coaches support teachers' increasing levels of expertise until they are comfortable with implementing and modifying the specified instructional practices on their own. In the coaching zone, literacy coaches stand ready to phase in to support the teacher and step back to let teachers interact independently with the students.

Coaching for Independence

Coaching for independence means that literacy coaches and teachers move beyond just the instructional practice. Thinking independently about instruction requires that the teachers feel comfortable making instructional adjustments as they teach and reflect on both their practice and their assumptions about literacy. Literacy coaches respond to teachers' queries, building up their independent thinking, and then withdraw their support as teachers become confident about using the newly suggested instructional procedures. Thus, the focal point of coaching is to empower teachers so they can carry out complex and multifaceted teaching actions on their own. With the support of the literacy coach, teachers can take control of their own learning. Thus, the literacy coach's work continues until teachers can improve student learning and create teaching modifications and actions on their own.

Selecting Examples to Support Teachers' Learning

Literacy coaches can support teachers' learning by selecting concrete examples from classroom interactions to promote conversations and collaborative reflections. These examples can expand the teachers' understanding (Lyons & Pinnell, 2001). While observing

Note 4.3 Using a Specific Example

As Fran was teaching, Karen watched the students as they responded. She was looking for a crucial incident that would demonstrate active reading. After the lesson, Karen retold an incident, highlighting significant aspects. She related to Fran this scenario: *After you read that section aloud and waited for responses, rather than asking a question about the story, you said, "Jeremy what are you thinking about your prediction?" Did you notice that Jeremy responded with two complete sentences? This was the most he has talked on topic.* Fran and Karen discussed how Jeremy and other students seemed to be actively engaged in thinking about this story. Discussing this incident helped Fran conceptualize active, engaged reading.

lessons, literacy coaches look for specific incidents within classroom interactions to demonstrate important aspects of student learning. When these teaching incidents occur, literacy coaches take careful notes to illustrate particular points about instruction; they later meet with the teachers to describe these incidents or scenes with essential details. Then, they lead the teachers' reflective thinking. Likewise, when teachers observe literacy coaches, they can select concrete examples to explain classroom interactions.

Literacy coaches and teachers use selected classroom examples to promote reflective conversations about the coherence between the teachers' personal views and their actual practice. Literacy coaches need to be attuned to teachers' practical reasoning so they can guide teachers to coherently connect their practice and their personal views.

Practical Reasoning

Coaching for independence develops practical reasoning. Each instructional experience adds to teachers' knowledge and views about literacy learning. As literacy coaches and teachers converse with each other, coaches can assist teachers as they clarify and reflect on their teaching. Instructional actions often appear spontaneous, but upon examination, they are rooted in practical reasoning and personal views. During these conversations, teachers build on and modify their own theoretical understanding of literacy and literacy learning. Consequently, as teachers change their practice, they also modify their views about literacy instruction and student learning.

Within practical reasoning, teachers focus on instructional events to construct their premises about literacy instruction. The gradual release of classroom coaching model usually includes several instructional events. Using these instructional events, literacy coaches help teachers reflect on and develop their views of literacy learning. Literacy coaches can use questions to encourage practical reasoning (see Table 4.3).

These comments or questions encourage teachers to rethink their practical assumptions about literacy learning. As coaches and teachers engage in reflective conversations, the teachers can flesh out the intuitive premises that guide their practice, thus increasing their ability to independently control their instructional decision making.

Table 4.3

Questions to Encourage Practical Reasoning

- How do these teaching experiences help you formulate your thinking?

- That's a very interesting way to think about . . . Can you explain your thinking?

- Can you point out an example that illustrates your thinking?

Collaborative Reflective Groups

Coaching for independence includes collaborative conversations that occur within reflective groups of teachers. During the discussions, teachers listen to each other closely, noting beliefs about students and literacy learning. The collaborative reflective group helps teachers reconsider not only their instruction but also their beliefs and values about teaching all students. In these groups, colleagues offer reflective comments to one another, which provides an opportunity to accept and challenge each others' thinking.

Teachers need continuous professional dialogue with other teachers to help focus their efforts, actions, and practice. Groups of colleagues are instrumental in creating a means for teachers to explore their personal assumptions and connect them to their teaching. Teachers come to a more informed understanding of their personal patterns of reasoning as they share them with others. Thus, these collaborative groups provide a means for teachers to continue their exploration of different instructional procedures. The shared responsibility for change involves literacy coaches and teachers who continually share reasoning and create options for teaching. Through this dialogue, teachers challenge each other to continue to enhance their teaching independent of the literacy coach.

Summary

The gradual release of classroom coaching model includes three phases to develop teacher learning. This model encourages teachers to take risks employing alternative instructional procedures. Teachers are provided with ongoing guided practice as they implement and modify specified instructional practices. Literacy coaches work to build up teachers' competence and confidence by modeling and then supporting attempts to implement suggested practices.

Observation, Analysis, and Interpretation

It is the theory that decides what can be observed.

Albert Einstein

Observations can reveal much about classroom interactions, but they can also provide a window into how teachers and literacy coaches think and develop their theories. Literacy coaches and teachers analyze and interpret their observations and reflections based on their personal theories of literacy learning. Like Einstein proposed, observations are critically related to the theory of literacy that teachers and coaches embrace. The observation, the analysis, and the interpretation add to the understanding of classroom interactions and the way teachers cope with different learners and situations. Thus, literacy coaches and teachers reflect on observations, student work, and conversations. In this book, literacy is viewed as an active-constructive process; that is, individuals use their knowledge and strategies to construct meaning with text.

There are many purposes for observing and analyzing student learning. The purposes for literacy coaching are to enhance student learning, create instructional adjustments, and extend professional development. These purposes do not require testing, nor are they aligned with accountability procedures. Literacy coaches and teachers are observing students construct meaning as they talk through their understanding, employ strategies and skills to build understanding, and engage with instructional events. These purposes require observations, analysis, and interpretations that inform literacy coaches and teachers about classroom interactions and student learning as a recurring routine. Instruction does not stop in order to test. It goes on.

Section 1
Observation

Observation is used as a tool to understand student learning and teacher development. Literacy coaches and teachers deliberately cultivate the habit of noticing and observing student learning and the teacher actions that produced it. These observations help them discuss observations within classroom interactions. During the preconference, literacy coaches and teachers identify specific aspects and teacher-student interactions they will jointly observe. Literacy coaches need to assure the teachers that the observations are made to inform instruction and guide their reflective conversations. The observations are not evaluative in nature. At the end of the observation, literacy coaches and teachers discuss their observations.

Observing lessons is a challenging task for literacy coaches. During observations, literacy coaches observe both the teachers' implementation of the instructional procedure and what students are actually learning. Literacy coaches note the specific areas that were designated to be watched in the preconference. In this way, they describe identified classroom interactions, teachers' actions, and student learning.

Conducting Observations

Observation is one approach that provides teachers and students with the information they need to enhance classroom interactions. Literacy coaches and teachers use an open format for writing observations and other methods to describe what occurs in the classroom. Narrative note taking, however, is a routine that captures rich descriptions of classroom learning.

Narrative Descriptions   Narrative descriptions describe teaching rather than evaluate it. Taking narrative notes supports the teacher-coach discussions and provides detailed information about what occurred in a classroom. Bean (2004) has suggested various observation routines that teachers and coaches can use. One process involves making a T-chart on a sheet of paper, labeling one side "Teacher" and the other side "Students." Literacy coaches record appropriate observations about the teacher and the students in their respective columns. Bean (2004) suggests drawing a line every five minutes so the observer can have a sense of the evolution of the interactions during the instructional event. Figure 5.1 shows an example chart.

Reviewing the notes shown in Figure 5.1, the literacy coach realizes this teacher is not using a constructive approach to teaching. The coach and the teacher discuss these observations and make a plan to modify the teacher's instruction. Another method is to use lines to note what happened before, during, and after the reading lesson. Using narrative note-taking, literacy coaches can capture both the teacher's instruction and the students' response.

Checklists   Although a complete narrative description is preferable, literacy coaches often need a little structure. Checklists can

Figure 5.1

T-Chart for Observations

Teacher	Students
Introducing new words by pointing, prompting to say & give definition.	Students are talking among each other.
Asks R-group to look closely at chart. Point at first wd. Redirects 4 times	They do have their books.
	S1 – reads dinosaur word quickly – he knows (it).
Gives silent "e" rule.	S2 – sounds word slowly – has difficulty w/ silent "e"
	S2 – Says the word correctly.
Ask S to read aloud	S3 – Rd aloud sounding Wds
Five minutes	
Ask R-group to discuss	Silence – eyes down or wandering
Ask predict	S4 – There's more about dinosaurs.
Teacher continues	
	S5 – Rd aloud--

be helpful because they are easy to craft and use. These lists can be useful for observing classroom interactions and quickly noting teachers' actions. At the same time, they are limited in that they do not provide information on the quality of the teachers' actions. They also must align closely with the research on effective classroom instruction. Thus, literacy coaches and teachers need to make sure the items on the checklist are based on research evidence. The checklist in Figure 5.2 was developed using the research on effective reading teachers (Taylor & Pearson, 2002; Taylor, Pearson, Peterson, & Rodriquez, 2003).

Observing Teachers

Observation of classroom interactions is an essential way to study how teachers teach. Literacy coaches note the teachers' actions and look for instructional moves that encourage student learning. Likewise, they observe the challenges the teachers encounter and the way teachers explain learning strategies and support student learning. As literacy coaches observe the lesson, they also might ask themselves the following questions:

- What kind of language is the teacher using?

- How does the teacher initiate discussion?

- Does the teacher ask all the questions?

- What kind of higher level questions does the teacher ask?

- How does the teacher reply to student responses?

- How much wait time does the teacher allow for student response?

- Does the teacher focus on what students are learning?

Figure 5.2

Checklist for Effective Teaching

Teacher's Name _____   Observer _____

Date _____   Beginning Time _____   Ending Time _____

For each observation, put checkmarks in the box.

Teacher Action	Numbers of Times Observed													
Provides many opportunities to engage in reading and writing.														
Focuses reading lesson on complete texts at an appropriate level.														
Engages students in constructing meaning as they read and write.														
Provides scaffolding during reading and writing instruction.														
Supports thinking rather than telling information.														
Focuses on higher level thinking during and after instruction.														
Provides for discussion of complete texts.														
Maintains high expectations for all students.														
Teaches strategies as well as skills in a constructivist manner.														
Provides opportunities to work in small groups or with a partner.														
Encourages individual responsibility in learning.														

Additionally, literacy coaches notice if the teacher shares and builds on responses and promotes higher order thinking. They also note potential places where the teacher could have made adjustments to increase student learning.

Observing Students

Student learning occurs as a result of multiple factors during classroom interactions. Both literacy coaches and teachers observe student learning as they try to capture the multiple influences that are involved. The knowledge about active readers and writers provides a backdrop for these observations. Literacy coaches and teachers can use the following questions related to active readers:

- Are students actively engaged?

- Do students talk within the classroom context?

- Are students constructing meaning?

- Are the students connecting text information with their prior knowledge?

- Are students verifying and checking their understanding?

- Are students elaborating upon what and how they read?

Literacy coaches and teachers observe students' literacy actions and write down significant aspects of their learning as well as concerns they have observed. Observing students is a key way to establish what students have learned in each lesson.

Observing Teacher-Student Interactions

Literacy coaches and teachers observe the interactions and the content of student and teacher talk. They also note the quality of the teacher-student interactions. Teacher-student interactions are a powerful influence on student learning (Johnston, 2003; Resnick & Junker, 2006). Teachers and literacy coaches should contemplate the following questions about teacher-student interactions:

- Do they discuss personal experiences and viewpoints?

- Do they discuss shared literacy experiences?

- Is there give and take in the conversations?

- What is the quality of the talk?

As literacy coaches observe the teacher-student interactions, they notice how much time the teacher focuses on maintaining attention and how much time the teacher spends discussing content. They also notice how much teacher talk and student talk is occurring. If teachers talk extensively, literacy coaches might suggest making a video recording of a lesson.

Observing and Collecting Student Work

As literacy coaches and teachers plan together, they decide on specific student actions they want to observe. Then, they decide if the students will create a product to illustrate their learning. If so, literacy coaches and teachers outline a way to collect the work. Looking at students' work can be one way to connect student learning with adaptations of literacy instruction.

Section 2
Analysis

Analysis involves the close examination of the observations made during the instructional event. During analysis, literacy coaches and teachers compare their observations with what they know about the active reading process. They analyze their observations by looking for patterns of actions that support the skillful use of the reading process.

Analyzing Teachers' Actions

Analyzing observations can contribute information teachers need about their practice. Teachers can talk with their literacy coach about the observations and then analyze them to plan modifications to their instructional practice. As literacy coaches and teachers analyze the teachers' actions, they refer to the questions that guided their observations (Lyons & Pinnell, 2001; Johnston, 2003). Together, the literacy coaches and the teachers analyze observations before, during, and after teaching the lesson.

Using Questions to Analyze Teachers' Actions The following questions present a framework for thinking about teachers' actions that could increase students' reading performance. As literacy coaches analyze observations, they think about what happened before the student began reading. They analyze how teachers:

Activate and develop background knowledge

Explain unfamiliar concepts and key vocabulary words

Engage and motivate students

After the introduction of the lesson, teachers and students read the story or passage, constructing meaning as they read. During reading, teachers make many moves in response to students' growing understanding. Both the literacy coaches and the teachers analyze how teachers:

Connect information to students' background knowledge

Make references to the text

Extend higher order thinking

Use prompts to stimulate thinking and learning

Adapt instruction to meet student challenges

Redirect students so their responses make sense

After the reading, the teachers and students react to and discuss the ideas they considered as they read. The literacy coaches analyze the teachers' actions and the teachers reflect on the lesson. After reading, literacy coaches and teachers rethink how understanding was supported. They both think about the students' learning by asking how the teachers supported students as they:

Elaborated background knowledge with new information

Connected important concepts

Expanded their strategy use

Engaged in discussion

These aspects help when analyzing the observations of the instructional event. Literacy coaches also ask questions to help teachers make connections between their observations and their own theories. They can ask:

"Is what you observed like something you know?"

"What makes you think that?"

"Can you tell me more about an observation?"

These questions help literacy coaches and teachers analyze observations about teacher actions.

Analyzing Teachers' Actions Using Rubrics Some coaches need a framework for specifically analyzing teachers' instruction. Rubrics that contain essential features for teaching a literacy lesson can be developed; however, it is difficult to create a rubric for such a complex task. These rubrics can be useful if coaches and teachers realize that there are ways to analyze teaching other than using benchmarks. There are several rubrics already developed for analyzing reading lessons. Lyons and Pinnell (2001) have developed an extensive evaluation system in their book *Systems for Change in Literacy Education: A Guide to Professional Development.*

Analyzing Student Learning

As literacy coaches and teachers analyze student learning, they refer to the questions that guided their observations. They consider their observations in light of the process of active reading. Readers talk about their understanding by engaging in social interactions that influence their meaning construction. Further, active readers construct meaning by intertwining text and background knowledge, monitoring their understanding and strategy use, and expanding what and how they read. Literacy coaches and teachers often ask questions about active reading as they analyze student observations.

Are Students Actively Engaged? Often, teachers think engagement is easy to observe, but students can obscure their wanderlust. Literacy coaches and teachers use their notes to specifically reflect on the amount of time the students were actually engaged in literate activities. They also look at various aspects of the lesson to describe student engagement as they ask:

Did the student understand the purpose of the lesson?

Was the student involved in the lesson introductions?

Was the student engaged during the reading of the text?

Was the student engaged during the discussion after reading?

Do Students Talk within the Classroom Context?

Thinking about this question, literacy coaches and teachers review their notes and rethink the conversations in the classroom. They analyze how each student contributed to the classroom talk. They ask themselves:

Did students talk in the discussions?

Was the talk on the topic or only tangential?

Did the students base their statements on evidence from the text?

Did others challenge them?

Did students modify their understanding?

These questions help teachers and literacy coaches analyze students' talk. They collaboratively discuss how the students' talk influenced the teachers' instruction and the students' learning.

Are Students Constructing Meaning Connecting the Text and Their Background Knowledge?

Teachers and literacy coaches look for patterns in the way students use both the text and their background knowledge. They describe what students refer to when responding during classroom interactions. Some students primarily rely on the text to form their understanding, whereas others use an abundance of prior knowledge rather than closely examining the text. These observations are considered in light of the other aspects of the students' active reading.

Are Students Verifying and Checking Their Understanding?

Using this question to analyze what was observed, teachers and literacy coaches look for evidence that the students were rethinking their responses. Students often pause to reflect on their thinking and ask themselves if what they are thinking fits with what they are reading. Sometimes, they rethink their responses because of teachers' prompts, but other times they rethink their understanding during classroom discussion as they respond to their classmates. In any event, literacy coaches and teachers look for clues that demonstrate the students were monitoring their understanding.

Are Students Elaborating What and How They Read?

Using their observations, literacy coaches and teachers look for examples in which students expanded their thinking about the topic. Frequently, students will elaborate on their own response or the responses of others. Thus, literacy coaches and teachers can review their notes on the discussion to focus on what strategies the students were using to elaborate on what they read.

As teachers and literacy coaches analyze student learning, they begin to share different perspectives about their observations. They ask themselves "What happened?" and "How does this relate to active reading?" Continually asking these questions causes teachers to be more responsive to students and their literate actions.

Analyzing Teacher-Student Interactions

Teacher-student interactions are a powerful influence for student learning (Johnston, 2003; Resnick & Junker, 2006). Observations are important, but analysis is extremely critical in order to improve teacher-student interactions. Because annotating all the interactions in a classroom is an impossible task, videotaping a lesson captures these teacher-student actions. Later, the literacy coach or the teacher can transcribe a section of the videotape. Transcribing a discussion provides fairly accurate information about the teacher-student interactions that might promote student learning. Teachers or literacy coaches can review the video recording, noting a section where there are a lot of teacher-student interactions as well as student-student interactions. They can then select five to ten minutes to analyze.

When analyzing the video, teachers can examine both their talk and the student responses. After teachers and literacy coaches transcribe the selected section, they can make a T chart that has teacher talk on one side and student talk on the other side (see Figure 5.3). This allows literacy coaches and teachers to visually analyze the amount of teacher talk and student talk. They also can

Figure 5.3

Excerpt from a Video Lesson Involving Three Struggling Readers

Teachers' Talk	Students' Talk
Student is reading aloud	S1 – "Whoa!! Sharp teeth the size of a banana!!!
Imagine those teeth	S2 – So I couldn't close my mouth.
You would have a mouthful	S3 – How much bananas??
One tooth was the size of the banana	S1 – So imagine they have 100 teeth
	S3 – Ahhh, the teeth are this big (shows with hands)

analyze teacher-student exchanges by examining what was said. Each exchange can be analyzed and placed in a category of talk such as: encouraging and scaffolding students' responses; weaving background knowledge into discussions; promoting complex language use; naming strategy use; asking higher level questions and fewer known answer questions; encouraging and modeling connection statements; challenging students to construct meaning rather than repeat answers, etc. (Goldenberg, 1992–1993; Johnston, 2003). Video recording teachers is a powerful way to analyze teacher-student interactions.

Analyzing Student Work

Analyzing student work has a profound impact on classroom learning (Checkley, 2000) because teachers recognize the connections between student learning and their actions. Learning to look at a piece of work in depth and describe what you see is an essential characteristic of analyzing and interpreting student work. Looking at students' work over time and engaging in reflective dialogue with others about the work are central aspects for analysis.

Note 5.1 Andrea, Juan, and Tanya, a Group of Third-Grade Teachers

In the case of the third-grade teachers, Andrea, Juan, and Tanya, who were working with story mapping and retelling, the teachers designed a rubric using a series of questions based on research evidence to evaluate their students' literacy learning. In individual conferences during the week, the teachers had the students retell a story, referring to their story map if needed. Andrea, Juan, and Tanya found that most of their students could retell stories. As a result, they changed their instruction using a lesson format of literature circles and discussion.

Searching for Patterns Some teachers arrange student work into categories based on learning goals: those that go beyond the learning goal, those that reach the goal, and those that do not reach the goal. In this process, they describe and explain the distinction among the groupings of student work. They ask one further question: Did anyone's work surprise me? Then they look for patterns within the groupings and individual student work to see what alternatives would develop student learning.

Using a Rubric Literacy coaches and teachers sometimes use rubrics so they can consistently evaluate student work. The rubric provides a scale to help ascertain the quality of specific aspects of a literacy task such as orally retelling a story or writing a summary of expository text.

The key aspects of the literacy task are described in detail, denoting differences between target performance and those that fall above or below this performance. Sometimes, a group of teachers may want to evaluate a specific literacy action such as a retelling. As in the creation of any other rubric, the teachers would use research on retelling to create a retelling rubric (see Table 5.1).

Section 3
Interpretation

Interpretation involves establishing the meaning of both the observations and analysis of an instructional event. Literacy coaches and teachers examine all the information they have collected and examine its meaning in light of literacy development, active reading, and the classroom situation.

Table 5.1

Retelling Rubric

	2	1	0
Setting	Has an elaborated explanation of setting, names major characters, important places and times	Has major character and briefly describes place and time	Contains only one idea, such as place, time, and/or names a character
Problem	Describes the major character's problem to be resolved, including theme	Names the main problem the major character needs to solve	Mentions the problem briefly
Events or Actions	Elaborates key story events related to resolving the problem	Names key story events	Names a few insignificant events
Resolution	Ends with a feeling of continuity elaborating how the problem was resolved	Briefly tells how the problem was resolved	Ends abruptly

Note: Adapted from Walker, Barbara J. (2008). *Diagnostic Teaching of Reading: Techniques for Instruction and Assessment*. Upper Saddle River, N.J.: Merrill/Prentice Hall/Pearson. Copyright 2008 by Pearson. Adapted by permission.

Interpretation of Classroom Interactions

Identifying specific observations and subsequent analysis, teachers and literacy coaches interpret what the teacher or student actions mean. This information is used to inform teachers' and coaches' decision making.

Interpreting Students' Actions Literacy coaches and teachers review their observations and analysis of student actions and work, and they ask the following: What do the students' actions and work reveal about their . . .

> understanding of the concept or topic?
>
> use of strategies and skills?
>
> next steps for instruction?

After discussing their responses to these questions, literacy coaches and teachers reflect on and record their interpretations in light of student learning.

Interpreting Teachers' Actions Literacy coaches review their observations and analysis of teachers' actions. They ask themselves and the teachers: What do the teachers' actions reveal about their:

> knowledge of literacy processes and active reading?
>
> knowledge of the specific instructional practice?
>
> knowledge of effective practices?
>
> knowledge of the classroom interactions?

After thinking about these questions, literacy coaches write down interpretations that make sense within the teachers' own knowledge. This information begins anew the coaching conversations and another preconference.

Interpreting Conversations

Conversations and interviews are valuable ways to understand both teacher and student learning. During many lessons, students talk about the strategies they use to construct meaning with text. However, often their responses depend on the questions the teachers ask. Teachers carefully craft their conversations and assignments to gather important information about student learning. Likewise, literacy coaches engage teachers in conversations about their practice. The conversations help the literacy coaches understand the teachers' instruction and their practical reasoning.

Conversational Interviews with Teachers During the preconference and postconference, literacy coaches talk with teachers about their instructional practices as well as their views about literacy and literacy instruction. These discussions reveal insights about the teachers' actions. The literacy coaches use the insights to reflect on the teachers' instruction and probe the teachers' thinking and planning. As teachers reflect on the questions coaches ask, they begin to think and talk about instructional strategies that enhance student learning.

Conversational Interviews with Students Asking students to talk about their literacy learning can reveal insights that teachers can use to plan and adapt instruction. As students and teachers

Note 5.2 John's Conversation

John, a third grader, once said to the teacher, "I'm not saying this in order." This revealed that John knew stories have a sequence, but he might not say a list of animals in order by the time he finished retelling. In other words, he knew what story development was and was not.

discuss literacy behaviors, students begin to think about how they read and write. Students may talk about their reading strategies and how they constructed meaning with text. Teachers frequently ask students about how their learning is progressing (Walker, 2008). They might inquire how often they use what they know to construct meaning and what strategies they use to develop word identification and text meaning. Further, they might ask students how they perceive themselves during discussions.

Students sometimes use self-correction strategies without telling the teacher, but when they are asked how they figured out an idea or a word, they immediately describe their thinking. Students may even offer these responses without prompting.

Student Conversations about Their Work Teachers often use students' work to focus their conversations with students. The students' work and the interviews become another way to derive information about classroom interactions. When students discuss their work with the teacher and literacy coach, they think about what a particular piece demonstrated about their reading and writing. With frequent inquiries, students become adept at responding with insightful information about their learning. In this way, they contribute to understanding learning in the classroom.

Summary

Learning to observe with inquisitive eyes and to note what is observed is another cornerstone of literacy coaching. Observations and the subsequent analysis inform instruction and student learning. Both observations and analysis provide ways to create powerful instructional modifications. Further analysis of student work can extend the insights developed through observations and analysis, as can conversations and interviews. Analyzing and interpreting all of these sources in light of active literacy and literacy development allows this information to be used to make informed classroom decisions and facilitate student learning.

Instructional Techniques Section

This section describes procedures for the various instructional techniques[1] discussed in this book. There are many other excellent resources that can be used for selecting instructional procedures.

In this book each instructional practice is divided into the steps of the procedure. This helps literacy coaches and teachers evaluate at what point during instruction the teacher modified instruction to increase student learning. The literacy coaches and teachers, then, reflect on reasons for deviating from the procedural steps.

The second half of the technique has been written for literacy coaches; however, it can help teachers, too. This part will help literacy coaches understand how the technique can be used successfully. Using this information will assist literacy coaches and teachers as they try to create instruction appropriate for the challenges the students are facing.

There are other books that provide instruction for literacy. The following lists a few of them:

---

[1] *Note:* The techniques have been adapted from Part II of *Diagnostic Teaching of Reading* (Walker, 2008). Used by permission.

Diagnostic Teaching: Techniques for Instruction and Assessment (Barbara J. Walker, 2008).

Multiple Pathways to Literacy: Assessments and Differentiated Instruction for Diverse Learners (Joan Gipe, 2006).

Strategies for Reading Assessment and Instruction (D. Ray Ruetzal and Robert B. Cooter, 2007).

Techniques for Reading Assessment and Instruction (Barbara J. Walker, 2005).

Directed Reading Thinking Activity

Description A directed reading thinking activity (DRTA) is an instructional format for teaching reading that includes predicting what the author will say, reading to confirm using the text, revising predictions, and elaborating understanding. Teachers and students discuss both understanding and strategy use.

Text Predominantly narrative texts

Procedure

1. The teacher asks students to predict what will happen in the story by looking at the title and any available pictures.

2. The students read until they get to a turning point in the story.

3. The teacher asks students whether their predictions were confirmed.

4. The teacher asks students to support their answers using the information in the text, and to explain their reasoning.

5. The teacher then asks the following questions:

 ■ What do you think is going to happen next?

 ■ Why do you think that?

6. The students read until they get to the next turning point in the story and the teacher repeats steps 3, 4, and 5, letting the students decide which information source they will use.

7. When they are finished reading, the teacher and students react to the story as a whole by discussing themes.

8. The teacher leads students in a discussion of the story, the author's purpose, and the strategies (confirming, summarizing, and prediction) they used to understand the story.

9. The teacher reviews the meaning of any key vocabulary words.

FOR THE LITERACY COACH

Basic View of Literacy Reading and writing are active thinking processes in which readers predict, confirm, and revise their writing and interpretation using important information. The reflective thought process focuses on not only what was understood but also how it was understood.

Pattern of Learner Strategies A DRTA is appropriate for students who readily engage in constructing meaning as they read. Readers use what they already know to predict what will happen and then select important information from the text to justify their responses. The teacher discusses not only what the students think but also how the students think.

For student observations, notice if:

1. The student directs and monitors his or her own learning when reading and writing.

2. The student uses appropriate resources (text-based, reader-based, etc.) when evaluating predictions.

3. The student is more comfortable retelling the story than answering questions.

For teacher observations, notice if:

1. The teacher explains and models, clearly demonstrating the processes of active literacy.

2. The teacher supports thinking by prompting.

3. The teacher phases in and models thinking aloud when necessary.

Evidence Base

Schorzman, E. M., & Cheek, E. Jr. (2004). Structured strategy instruction: Investigating an intervention for improving sixth-graders' reading comprehension. *Reading Psychology, 25,* 37–60.

Graphic Organizers

Description Graphic organizers are designed to provide a visual representation of the key words in content-area reading. By conceptually arranging the key words in a chapter, the teacher and students develop a conceptual framework for relating unfamiliar and familiar vocabulary words and concepts.

Text Predominantly expository text

Procedure

1. The teacher chooses a chapter from a textbook.

2. The teacher selects key vocabulary words and concepts.

3. The teacher selects a graphic organizer to fit the vocabulary word or concepts.

4. The teacher arranges the key words or concepts on the diagram to show the relationships among the key words and concepts.

5. The teacher adds a few familiar words to the diagram so students can connect their prior knowledge with the new information.

6. The teacher presents the selected graphic organizer on a chalkboard, overhead transparency, or PowerPoint slide. As the teacher presents the organizer, he or she explains the relationships. A structured overview is shown as an example.

7. Students are encouraged to explain how they think the information is related.

8. The students read the chapter, referring as needed to the graphic organizer.

9. After reading the selection, the students may return to the graphic organizer to clarify and elaborate concepts.

Figure 0.1

Graphic Organizer of Word Meaning

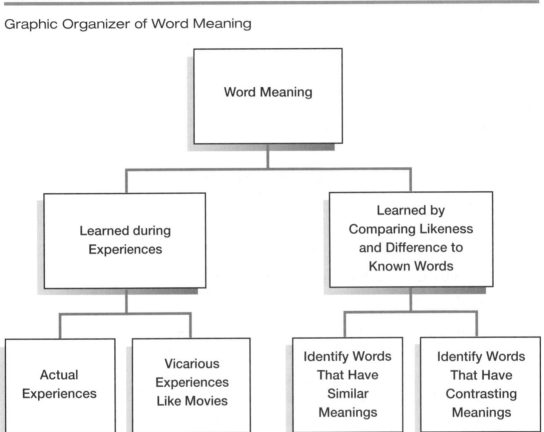

FOR THE LITERACY COACH

Basic View of Literacy Literacy is an active process in which learners use what they know to elaborate and extend what they write and what the text says. By constructing a visual map of word relationships, the teacher helps to create an idea framework prior to reading and writing.

Pattern of Learner Strategies The graphic organizer technique is appropriate for students who profit from a visual framework that relates unfamiliar words and ideas to known information. It is especially useful for those students who profit from visually conceptualizing relationships.

For student observations, notice if:

1. The student can easily detect the visual relationships among key words.

2. The student refers to the graphic organizer as he or she reads.

3. The student can organize the information learned.

For teacher observations, notice if:

1. The teacher clearly explains and discusses the relationships demonstrated by the graphic organizer.

2. The teacher has the students discuss the relationships.

3. The teacher refers to the textual information related to the graphic organizer.

Evidence Base

DiCecco, V. M., & Gleason, M. M.(2002). Using graphic organizers to attain relational knowledge from expository text. *Journal of Learning Disabilities, 35,* 306–320.

Robinson, D. H., & Kiewra, K. A.(1995). Visual argument: Graphic organizers are superior to outlines in improving learning from text. *Journal of Educational Psychology, 87,* 455–467.

Interactive Writing (Grades K–2)

Description   Interactive writing is a collaboration among teachers and their students in which they jointly write a passage. The teachers model writing words as they ask students what sounds they hear in the words. The teachers help students connect those sounds with corresponding letters and then write the words as they talk aloud about the sounds. The teachers and students share the pen when writing words.

Text   Collaborative teacher and student written text

Procedure

1. The teacher and students jointly discuss the topic and decide what to write. As they compose the text or story, the teacher acts as the facilitator, modeling, adding, summarizing, and combining the students' ideas.

2. As the students begin orating another story or retelling a familiar story, the teacher begins writing and talking aloud about the words they are writing.

3. The teacher asks some students to take over writing the next couple of words as the other students continue telling the story.

4. The teacher "takes the pen back" and talks aloud about the sounds as he or she spells the next word.

5. The teacher invites another student to continue writing the letters as all students sound out the words and the selected student writes the word as it is spelled aloud.

6. As students are writing the words, the teacher discusses the words. The students and teacher alternately share the pen.

7. When the story is completely written, the teacher reads the story as a whole and discusses story construction.

FOR THE LITERACY COACH

View of Literacy Reading and writing are socio-interactive processes in which the students' ideas and knowledge about written conventions can be learned through group interactions and teacher modeling. Through writing, the students become sensitive to written conventions such as letter formation, phonics, spelling, and sentence sense as well as how stories are constructed so that they make sense.

Pattern of Learner Strategies Interactive writing is most appropriate for all students, but is particularly suitable for students who have facility with telling a story and who like to write. This approach helps students develop a sense of the language structures and approach text as a communication between reader and writer.

For student observations, notice if:

1. The student can form some of the letters, knows letter names and some letter sounds.

2. The student prefers to write sounds rather hear sounds in words.

3. The student can talk about the written conventions.

For teacher observations, notice if

1. The teacher clearly models, thinking aloud about spelling as he or she writes each letter.

2. The teacher discusses the whole word and uses it in a sentence and establishes meaning.

3. The teacher discusses word meaning and the way the word fits into the overall passage or sentence.

Evidence Base

Craig, S. A. (2003). The effects of an adapted interactive writing intervention on kindergarten children's phonological awareness, spelling, and early reading development *Reading Research Quarterly, 38,* 438–440.

Retelling

Description Retelling is a technique in which a reader talks through the story in an organized format, discussing the characters, setting, problems, main episodes, and resolution.

Text Narrative

Procedure

1. Before reading, the teacher explains to the students that they will be asked to orally retell the story as if they were telling it to a friend who has never heard it before.

2. After reading, the students tell the story, noting the important parts: setting, characters, theme, plot, episodes, and resolution.

3. If the student is hesitant, the teacher uses prompts at the beginning, middle, and end like: "Once there was . . . who did . . . in the. . . . (The character) had a problem. . . . To solve the problem, (the character does . . .) . . . first . . . second . . . third. . . . Finally, the problem was solved by . . . and then. . . ."

4. The teacher can use illustrations or have students draw story events before retelling.

5. When the retelling is complete, the teacher can ask direct questions about important information omitted.

FOR THE LITERACY COACH

Basic View of Literacy Reading and writing are socio-interactive processes in which the students reconstruct the story, thinking about what they want to communicate to the instructional group. Their interpretation includes their own perceptions of what is important.

Pattern of Learner Strategies The retelling approach is most appropriate for students who have verbal strengths and can remember the story long enough to internalize it and retell it. Retelling uses their strength to expand textual information.

For student observations, notice if:

1. The student can verbalize some ideas about the story.

2. The student organizes a response that includes some of the story elements.

3. The student can end the retelling with a conclusion related to solving problems.

For teacher observations, notice if:

1. The teacher uses clear explanations and notices whether students understand the story.

2. The teacher is responsive to students, providing hints and prompts.

3. If necessary, the teacher models the retelling.

Evidence Base

Gambrell, L. B., Koskinen, P. S., & Kapinus, B. A. (1991). Retelling and the reading comprehension of proficient and less-proficient readers. *Journal of Educational Research, 84,* 356–362.

Semantic Mapping

Description Semantic mapping or webbing develops understanding by visually mapping relationships among words and ideas. The target idea or word is placed in the center of a circle. The students brainstorm information they already know about the word or idea. The students' knowledge and new information are arranged around this target idea to show relationships between what students already know and the new word or idea.

Text Key words or ideas (often used to introduce vocabulary words for a passage or story)

Procedure

1. The teacher chooses a word or idea that is a key aspect of what is to be read.

2. The teacher writes the word inside a circle in the middle of a blank page, chalkboard, or PowerPoint slide.

3. The students and teacher brainstorm what is already known about this word or idea and place the information in meaningful categories around the word, making a visual array of the relationships.

4. The teacher adds each new idea or word that describes the target idea to the web by drawing lines and new circles that indicate their relationships (see the Figure 0.2).

5. The students read the story.

6. The students and the teacher add additional information to the semantic map.

7. The students and the teacher discuss new understandings, relating them to known concepts and new relationships that were discovered during reading.

FOR THE LITERACY COACH

Basic View of Literacy Reading and writing are interactive processes in which students use their background knowledge to create semantic relationships between words (verbal labels) and world knowledge (big ideas). After reading, they extend their new learning by drawing relationships among what they learned and the original map.

Pattern of Learner Strategies Semantic mapping encourages students to use their experiential knowledge to expand their understanding; therefore, it is most appropriate for students who tend to think about relationships without describing these relationships in

Figure 0.2

Semantic Map of Comprehension

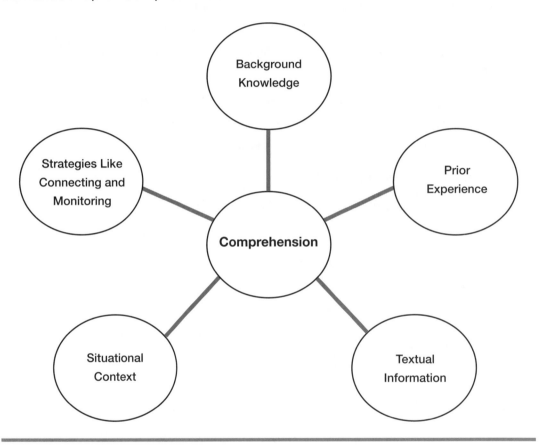

words. This strategy facilitates learning because it begins by show-
ing the visual relationships and then uses words to explain those
relationships.

For student observations, notice if:

1. The student uses the map to make verbal connections with personal experiences.

2. The student often has a general understanding but does not know specific words, and mapping helps to express that understanding.

3. The student's elaboration of ideas is marked with the word *thing* instead of a specific word.

For teacher observations, notice if:

1. The teacher brainstorms what the students already know and writes everyone's response on the chalkboard or semantic map.

2. The teacher makes comments on the relationships of the ideas mapped.

3. The teacher reviews the map and adds information during the discussion after reading.

Evidence Base

Bimmel, P. E., van den Bergh, H., Utrecht, U., & Oostdam, R. J. (2001). Effects of strategy training on reading comprehension in first and foreign language. *European Journal of Psychology of Education, 16,* 509–529.

Ruddell, R. B., & Boyle, O. F. (1989). A study of cognitive mapping as a means to improve summarization and comprehension of expository text. *Reading Research and Instruction, 29,* 12–22.

Story Mapping

Description Story mapping is a visual representation of the logical sequence of events in a narrative text. The elements of setting, character, problem, goal, events, and resolution are recorded visually on a sheet of paper.

Text Any narrative text with a fairly coherent story line

Procedure

1. The teacher selects a narrative passage of sufficient length so that it has a cohesive story line.

2. The teacher discusses the organization of a story by explaining that every story has a beginning, middle, and end.

   a. The beginning tells the place and who the characters are.

   b. During the middle of the story, the central character has a problem and makes a plan to solve it. Certain events in the story lead to solving the problem.

   c. The end of the story tells how the character(s) solved the problem.

3. The teacher explains the visual story map (see the accompanying figure) and relates it to story organization.

4. The students read the story.

5. The teacher and students fill out the map together. The teacher prompts when necessary.

Figure 0.3

Story Map of The Ugly Duckling

Setting: *Near a pond*
Characters: *mother duck and her ducklings*

Problem:
One duckling is really ugly and doesn't fit in.

Event:
The eggs hatch and there is one duckling that is different.

Event:
As this duckling grows up it gets teased a lot for being different. He cries and walks off.

Event:
The ugly duckling runs into other baby swans and these ducklings look like him. The mother swan takes care of the ugly duckling.

Resolution:
The ugly duckling grows up to be a beautiful swan and has a place to belong.

FOR THE LITERACY COACH

Basic View of Literacy Reading and writing are interactive processes in which the students construct meaning by thinking about the elements of a story to help them comprehend the theme or main idea of the story.

Pattern of Learner Strategies Story mapping is most appropriate for the learner who profits from a visual representation of story organization in order to develop adequate comprehension. Often the abundance of facts overwhelms young students, who need a simple structure such as a story map to apply to stories.

For student observations, notice if:

1. The student understands the story map elements.

2. The student improves his or her ability to retell the story.

3. The student improves his or her ability to answer questions about story events.

For teacher observations, notice if:

1. The teacher clearly explains all elements of the story map.

2. The teacher models how to fill out the story map after he or she explains the procedure.

3. The teacher scaffolds learning for students who have difficulty understanding story elements.

Evidence Base

Mathes, Patricia G., Fuchs, Douglas, & Fuchs, Lynn S. (1997). Cooperative story mapping. *Remedial and Special Education, 18,* 20–27.

Davis, Zephaniah T. (1994). Effects of prereading story mapping on elementary readers' comprehension. *Journal of Educational Research, 87,* 353–360.

Summary Experience Approach

Description The teacher and students talk about the classroom story. Based on the classroom reading material, the students are asked to retell the story while the teacher records or writes down the retelling. This summary (dictated retelling) becomes material that is read by the student.

Text Students' dictated summaries

Procedure

1. The teacher engages the students in discussion about the classroom reading selection.

2. The students are asked to retell the classroom selection while the teacher serves as a secretary and writes down what the students say.

3. Using leading questions, the teacher guides the students to retell the selection by using questions such as: What happened next? What are the important parts? How does the passage end? (For additional prompts, see "Retelling" in this part.)

4. The students and teacher read the dictated summary together to revise any statements or phrases that are unclear. They also check to see if the summary follows the natural language patterns of the students.

5. The teacher and students read the summary repeatedly so that the repetition of the summary helps the students recognize the words.

6. The summary is written on a sheet of paper or word processed. The teacher makes several copies. Thus, the students can take one copy home to practice.

7. The teacher and students create a book of story summaries.

FOR THE LITERACY COACH

Basic View of Literacy Reading and writing are active, learner-based processes. By writing and then reading their own summary, the students will learn the key vocabulary words from the classroom story. Because the summary is short and uses their own language structures, the students will be able to figure out and remember the words in the summary, which will, in turn, facilitate understanding of the classroom stories.

Patterns of Learner Strategies The summary experience approach is most appropriate for students who have facility with language and have difficulty reading words and understanding meaning. If students use their own language to retell the story, then the summary experience matches their language patterns.

For student observations, notice if:

1. The student can retell the main actions of the story.

2. The student can remember how he or she retold the story well enough to predict the words he or she does not remember.

3. The student deciphers a word when prompted, using what he or she said in the summary and the story theme.

For teacher observations, notice if:

1. The teacher prompts students to include elements of the story map.

2. The teacher prompts students as they reread the summary experience using cues like "Do you remember what the classroom story is about?" or "How did you say that in your story?"

3. The teacher provides task-related comments such as "You really understood the main character" and "You described the characters in great detail."

Evidence Base

Daisey, P. (2000). The construction of "How To" books in a secondary content area literacy course: The promise and barriers of writing to learn strategies. In P. E. Linder, W. M Linek, E. G. Sturtevant. & J. R. Dugan (Eds.), *Literacy at a new horizon* (pp. 147–159). Commerce, TX: College Reading Association.

Palinscar, A. S., Parecki, A. D., & McPhail, J. C. (1995). Friendship and literacy through literature. *Journal of Learning Disabilities, 28,* 503–510.

Think-Aloud Approach

Description The think-aloud approach uses the students' thinking to develop active reading. By following the sequence of self-directed questions, the students learn to monitor their understanding and self-regulate their understanding.

Text Narrative and expository texts

Procedure

1. The teacher decides to think aloud, predicting and revising understanding.

2. The teacher selects a text that is at the appropriate level and has a fairly cohesive story line.

3. The teacher decides on key prediction points. A story map (see "Story Mapping" in this part) can facilitate this process.

4. The teacher begins by modeling how to think through the story, asking:

   "What must I do? . . . I must guess what the author is going to say. . . . A good strategy is to use the title. . . . From the title, I predict that this selection is about . . ."

5. Using another section of the story, the teacher models a plan for predicting:

   "Now, let's see. What's my plan for predicting? . . . To make my prediction, I already know that . . . To prove my guess, I must look for hints in the text . . ."

6. The teacher writes these two aspects on a chalkboard:

   "I already know. . . . Hints from the text . . ."

7. Then, the teacher answers the question

   "Does my prediction fit with the text clues and what I know about them?"

"I wonder how it fits? . . . The _____ must be impor-tant because the author keeps talking about it. . . . It fits because _____."

8. Using other sections of the story, the teacher writes "Oops" on the chalkboard while he or she models correction strat-egies by saying:

   "Oops, that doesn't make sense. . . . I need to check my think-ing. . . . So far, I'm right about . . . but wrong about . . ."

9. As the teacher models this strategy, he or she also models self-talk related to making a mistake by saying:

   "It's okay to make a mistake. . . . I can change my predic-tion as I get more information. From the new information, I predict that . . . or I wonder whether . . ."

10. Using another section, the teacher models tentative thinking by saying, "Hmmmm" and writing it on the chalkboard:

    "Hmmm. Sometimes, I am just not sure. . . . Maybe it's . . . or maybe it's . . ."

11. The teacher models confirming predictions by saying, "I knew it, that sure fits. . . . So far I'm on the right track . . ."

12. The teacher writes, "I knew it" on the chalkboard. The stu-dents and teacher return to step 4 and think aloud about another section of the story.

13. Students read a different section of the story and then think aloud.

14. When students' thinking doesn't fit, the teacher models his or her own thinking rather than asking questions, saying, "When I read that passage, I thought . . ."

15. At the end of the story, the students and the teacher discuss the story content and how they constructed meaning.

FOR THE LITERACY COACH

Basic View of Literacy   Reading and thinking are interactive processes in which the students build their understanding based on text and what they know. As students build an understanding, they predict, monitor, and elaborate their learning.

Pattern of Learner Strategies   The think-aloud approach is most appropriate for students who use too much of what they know, failing to monitor reading comprehension and to relate textual information to prior knowledge. For these students, the approach matches their strong strategy of using prior knowledge and helps them revise their understanding based on textual information.

For student observations, notice if:

1. The student can make a prediction.

2. The student can follow the oral discussion of strategic reading and writing.

3. The student learns to use key events to predict outcomes.

For teacher observations, notice if:

1. The teacher explains and models clearly, demonstrating the process of active reading.

2. The teacher phases in and models thinking aloud when necessary.

3. As students develop self-regulated strategies, the teacher supports thinking by prompting.

Evidence Base

Baumann, J. F., Seifert-Kessell, N.,& Jones, L. A. (1992). Effect of think-aloud instruction on elementary students' comprehension monitoring abilities. *Journal of Reading Behavior, 24,* 143–172.

Walker, B. (2005). Thinking aloud: Struggling readers often require more than a model. *The Reading Teacher, 58,* 688–692.

Study Guide Section

Literacy Coaching:
Learning to Collaborate

Teachers can use this book for a coach's study group. Study Groups are described in Chapter 2. To begin, group members study the principles of collaboration so they are free to share thoughts and perspectives about the content of *Literacy Coaching: Learning to Collaborate.* To get the book study started, group members need to know something about each other. Bringing an artifact that demonstrates one's strengths, experiences, or goals is one way to do this. After discussion starts, it is everyone's responsibility to keep the discussion moving. I have included questions and activities (Birchak, Connor, Crawford, Kahn, Kaser, Turner, & Short, 1998) that have been adapted to deal with the content of the book. In addition to these, there are ways to keep the conversation moving by taking turns and asking each other about ideas. These procedures and questions follow:

1. Restating ideas to clarify understanding and to highlight the important points. Questions might begin with "So are you saying . . . ?"

2. Asking questions to encourage deeper thinking. Use questions like: "Can you tell me more?" and "How important is that to you?"

3. Encouraging reflection about important ideas.

4. Encouraging rethinking previous comments. "Last week you brought up the issue of _____. I want to talk more about that."

5. Keeping the discussion moving. Focus on what the person is saying and use language that opens conversations like "I might . . ." or "I wonder. . . ."

These questions will help advance the book study discussion.

Keeping a journal about your ideas will increase your participation. In the journal, you can write group questions and other information that is important to you. The first entry for each chapter might be the important ideas of the chapter. The following questions have been prepared for a study group (book) discussion.

Chapter 1
Literacy Coaching in a Learning Community

1. Write two questions and find one phrase to use during the discussion.

2. Of the three coaching models, which one do you prefer, and why?

3. According to Walker, what is a learning community? Explain key interactions that promote the community.

4. Describe your knowledge about literacy processes, development, and instruction. What else do you need to learn about literacy?

5. Describe and discuss the interdependent relationship among the literacy coach, the teacher, and the student.

6. Walker discussed three knowledge bases that literacy coaches need. Explain those knowledge bases. Discuss other understandings that literacy coaches might need.

7. Discuss practical reasoning. Think of a recent instructional lesson. What are some rationales or reasons you use to explain your teaching?

8. Go to the website below and read one short article to share with the study group. Talk about how the article relates to the first chapter.
   http://www.literacycoachingonline.org/briefs.html

Chapter 2
Coaching and Collaboration

1. Choose a favorite quote from this chapter. Share it with the study group and tell why you chose it.

2. Walker lists several attributes of collaboration. Are there others you would add to the list?

3. How is collaboration different from cooperation? Compare and contrast these concepts.

4. What does *sharing perspectives* mean? How often do you share your perspectives about literacy learning?

5. According to Walker, what are the purposes of the small collaborative groups? How would they help student learning?

6. How are reflective discussion groups and teacher research groups alike? How are they different?

7. If you were choosing a book for a study group, what would you select and why?

8. Discuss how the following web article relates to this chapter. Go to http://www.centerforcsri.org/index. php?Itemid=5&id=436&option=com_content&task=view

Chapter 3
The Cycle of Literacy Coaching

1. Think about your strengths as a teacher. Discuss one of your strengths with the study group.

2. What are the characteristics of a coaching conversation? Share with the study group a professional conversation you have had. Does it have the same characteristics as a coaching conversation? How was it similar or different?

3. Thinking about the preconference, would you jointly make all the selections recommended? Why or why not?

4. Is personal reflection an important part of the instructional event? If so, what are the benefits of personal reflection?

5. The coaching cycle has three broad aspects—the preconference, the instructional event, and the postconference. Choose a personal experience that explains one aspect.

6. Reflect on formal theories of literacy learning, and explain how they relate to your practice. Why is it important to relate practical reasoning to formal theories?

7. Review the chapter and think about three personal teaching experiences related to the chapter content. Describe the personal experiences and have the group collaboratively reflect with you about what to do next.

8. Go to the literacy coaching resources page designated below and click on Supporting the Role of the Reading Coach. On page 16, there is a cycle of coaching. Compare this cycle to the one described by Walker
http://www.literacycoachingresources.info/
ResourcesonCoachin.html

Chapter 4
The Gradual Release Model of Literacy Coaching

1. Write three open-ended questions about Chapter 4. Ask them when appropriate.

2. What does modifying instruction mean? How does it help student learning?

3. Thinking about your own expertise, which coaching procedures would you use the most? Are you comfortable implementing all of them?

4. Reread the example of Karen modeling active reading. How does modeling promote student learning? What else could have helped Fran understand the instructional process?

5. What happens during "Coaching in the Zone"? Choose one strategy in this section and explain it to the group.

6. Explain how practical reasoning is part of "Coaching for Independence." How does it develop teacher knowledge?

7. As a group, choose an instructional technique. In groups of three, let one person be the teacher, another the coach, and the third a reader and implement a lesson. Discuss the experience in the study group.

8. Go to the website below to read the first chapter of *Better Learning Through Structured Teaching: A Framework for the Gradual Release of Responsibility* by Douglas Fisher and Nancy Frey (2008). In searching for the chapter, click on sample chapters, then choose the letter "b," and then look for the title and click. Explain what you learned. http://www.ascd.org/portal/site/ascd/menuitem. 7ecb0460a2b144dd12c7c91061a001ca/

Chapter 5
Observation, Analysis, Interpretation

1. Describe your favorite teacher/coach conversation. Can any aspect of the conversation inform teacher practice?

2. As a group, explain the process of observing, analyzing, and interpreting. How are these processes related?

3. From the continuing assessment tools described in this chapter, choose one to describe to the group.

4. Make an observation of a conversation, student-teacher interaction, student action, or teacher action. Discuss this observation with the group.

5. Study and reflect on the "Checklist for Effective Teaching of Reading." Use the checklist to evaluate yourself or another teacher.

6. Bring an example of student work to discuss with the study group. Have all members look at the piece of work and describe what the student is able to do and what he or she might need to work on. Using the questions in the chapter, prepare a question to focus comments such as "What are the strengths you see in the students' summaries?"

7. Conversational interviews are an integral part of the information a literacy coach has about teachers and students. How can this information be used to interpret teaching literacy and learning literacy?

8. Go to the Rubistar website (http://rubistar.4teachers.org/ index.php) and create a rubric for an assignment you are doing in your classroom. If you don't have a classroom, then you can make a rubric for discussion. Use the discussion rubric to evaluate your study group.

Instructional Techniques Section

The Instructional Techniques Section includes only those techniques that were used in the classroom examples in this book. The following questions and activities involve some of the techniques and the content of the entire book.

1. There are many pathways for learning to read and write. Describe your favorite instructional technique to the study group.

2. In Chapter 3, explain why Gail, the literacy coach, suggested story mapping to help the students to learn to retell the story.

3. Review the case in which Karen and Fran used the Think-aloud procedure. Think about Jeremy. How did this technique advance his comprehension?

4. Make a graphic organizer of how you would think about literacy coaching. Use information from the chapters to build an organizer. For various models, see the website below. http://www.educationoasis.com/curriculum/ graphic_organizers.htm

5. Discuss the following quote in relation to what you have learned in this book. What does literacy coaching have to do with systems thinking?

Systems thinking is a discipline for seeing wholes. It is a framework for seeing interrelationships rather than things, for seeing patterns of change rather than static "snapshots."

—Peter Senge

References

Bean, R. (2004). *The reading specialist: Leadership for the classroom, school, and community.* New York: Guilford Press.

Birchak, B., Connor, C., Crawford, K. M., Kahn, L., Kaser, S., Turner, S., & Short, K. G. (1998). *Teacher study groups: Building community through dialogue and reflection.* Champaign, IL: National Council of Teachers of English.

Braunger, J., & Lewis, J. P. (2005). *Building a knowledge base in reading* (2nd ed.). Newark, DE: The International Reading Association and The National Council of English.

Checkley, K. (2000). Learning to look: Analyzing student work to improve teacher practice. *Classroom Leadership, 3,* 115–117.

Costas, A. R., & Garmston, R. J. (2002). *Cognitive coaching: A foundation for renaissance schools.* Norwood, MA: Christopher Gordon Publishing.

Dozier, C. (2006). *Responsive literacy coaching: Tools for creating and sustaining purposeful coaching.* Portland, ME: Stenhouse Publications.

DuFour, Richard (2004). Leading edge: Culture shift doesn't occur overnight—or without conflict. *Journal of Staff Development, 25,* 29–34.

Freire, P. (1970/2005). *Pedagogy of the oppressed* (30th Anniversary ed.). New York: Continuum.

Gambrell, L. B., Malloy, J. A., & Mazzoni, S. A.(2006). Evidence-based best practices for comprehensive literacy instruction. In L. B. Gambrell, L. M. Morrow, & M. Pressley (Eds.) *Best practices in literacy instruction* (3rd ed., pp. 11–29). New York: Guilford Press.

Goldenberg, C. (1992–1993). Instructional conversations: Promoting comprehension through discussion. *The Reading Teacher, 46,* 316–326.

Grinder, M. (1996). *Envoy: Your personal guide to classroom management.* Battle Ground, WA: Michael Grinder Associates.

Guthrie, J. T., & Wigfield, A. (2000). Engagement and motivation in reading. In M. L. Kamil, P. B. Mosenthal, P. D. Pearson, & R. Barr (Eds.), *Handbook of reading research: Volume III* (pp. 403–422). New York: Erlbaum.

Holdzkom, D. (2001). *Low performing schools: So you've identified them—now what?* Charleston, WV: Appalachia Educational Laboratory.

International Reading Association. (2004). *The role and qualifications of the Reading Coach in the United States. Position Statement.* Newark, DE.

Johnston, P. (2003). *Choice words: How our language affects children's learning.* Portland, ME: Stenhouse.

Kennedy, M. (1998, April). *The relevance of content in inservice teacher education.* Paper presented at the annual meeting of the American Educational Research Association.

Lyons, C. A., & Pinnell, G. S. (2001). *Systems for change in literacy education: A guide to professional development.* Portsmouth, NH: Heinemann.

Neufeld, B., & Roper, D. (2003). *A strategy for developing instructional capacity: Promises and practicalities.* Downloaded on December 15, 2006, http://www.annenberginstitute.org/images/Coaching.pdf

McLaughlin, M. W., & Talbert, J. E. (2001). *Professional communities and the work of high school teaching.* Chicago: University of Chicago Press.

McLaughlin, M., & Talbert, J. (2006). *Building school-based teacher learning communities: Professional strategies to improve student achievement.* Columbia, NY: Teachers College Press.

Mraz, M., Algozzine, B., & Watson, P. (2008). Perceptions and expectations of roles and responsibilities of literacy coaching. *Literacy Research and Instruction, 47,* 141–157.

Pearson, P. D., & Gallagher, M. C. (1983). The instruction of reading comprehension. *Comtemporary Educational Psychology, 8,* 317–344.

Poglinco, S. M., Bach, A. J., Hovde, K., Rosenblum, S., Saunders, M., & Supovitz, J. A. (2003). *The heart of the matter: The coaching model in America's Choice schools.* Philadelphia: University of Pennsylvania, Consortium for Policy Research in Education. Retrieved September 12, 2006, from www.cpre.org/Publications/AC-06.pdf

Rasinski, T. (2003). *The fluent reader.* New York: Scholastic.

Resnick, L., & Junker, B. (2005). *Using the instructional quality assessment toolkit to investigate the quality of reading comprehension assignments and student work.* Los Angeles: The Regents of the University of California.

Richardson, V., & Anders, P. L. (2005). Professional preparation and development of teachers in literacy instruction for urban settings. In J. Flood & P. L. Anders, *Literacy development of students in urban schools: Research and policy.* Newark, DE: International Reading Association.

Rosemary, C., Roskos, K., & Landreth, L.(2007). *Designing professional development in literacy: A framework for effective instruction.* New York: Guilford Press.

Roskos, K., & Walker, B. J. (1994). *Interactive handbook for understanding reading diagnosis.* Upper Saddle River, NJ: Merrill/ Prentice Hall.

Sturtevant, E. (2003). *A key to improving teaching and learning in secondary schools.* Alliance for Excellent Education.

Taylor, B., & Pearson, P. D. (2002). *Teaching reading: Effective schools, accomplished teachers.* Mahwah, NJ: Lawrence Erlbaum.

Taylor, B., Pearson, P. D., Peterson, D. S., & Rodriquez, M. C. (2003). Reading growth in high-poverty classrooms: The influence of teacher practices that encourage cognitive engagement in literacy learning. *The Elementary School Journal, 104,* 3–28.

Toll, C. (2005). *The literacy coach's survival guide: Essential questions and practical answers.* Newark, DE: International Reading Association.

Toll, C. (2008). *Surviving but not yet thriving: Essential questions and practical answers for experienced literacy coaches.* Newark, DE: International Reading Association.

Vygotsky, L. S. (1978). *Mind in society.* Cambridge, MA: Harvard University Press.

Walker, B. (2008). *Diagnostic teaching of reading: Techniques for instruction and assessment* (6th ed.). Upper Saddle River, NJ: Merrill/Pearson.

Walker, B., Scherry, R., & Gransberry, C. (2001). Collaboration in the schools: A theoretical and practical view. In V. Risko & K. Bromley (eds.) *Collaboration for Diverse Learners: Viewpoints and Practices.* Newark, DE: International Reading Association.

Wilson, S., & Berne, J. (1999). Teacher learning and the acquisition of professional knowledge: An examination of research on contemporary professional development. In A. Iran-Nejad & P.D. Pearson (Eds.), *Review of research in education* (No. 24, pp. 173–209). Washington, DC: American Educational Research Association.

Index